Living
out the life of Jesus

The fruit of the Spirit

Florence MacKenzie

Scripture Union, 207–209 Queensway, Bletchley, MK2 2EB, England.
email: info@scriptureunion.org.uk
web site: www.scriptureunion.org.uk

We are an international Christian charity working with churches in more than 130
countries providing resources to bring the good news about Jesus Christ to children,
young people and families – and to encourage them to develop spiritually through the
Bible and prayer.

As well as our network of volunteers, staff and associates who run holidays, church-
based events and school Christian groups, we produce a wide range of publications
and support those who use our resources through training programmes.

First published 2002

ISBN 1 85999 430 X

British Library Cataloguing-in-Publication Data

A catalogue record for this book is available from the British Library.

Cover design: Carsten Lorenz

Printed in Great Britain by Ebenezer Baylis & Son Ltd, The Trinity Press, Worcester
and London.

Contents

Introduction 5

How to use this study 7

Notes for leaders 8

1 Love 10

2 Joy 17

3 Peace 23

4 Patience 30

5 Kindness 38

6 Goodness 45

7 Faithfulness 51

8 Gentleness 59

9 Self-control 66

10 Keep growing! 74

Endnotes 82

To
Helen, Lesley, Margaret, Matti,
May, Meg, Nicola and Susan,
whose enthusiasm, support and encouragement
have been God's gift to me as we field-tested this
study together for his glory.

Introduction

Let me ask you a question – are you able to list the fruit of the Spirit mentioned in Galatians 5:22,23? Here's a second question – is this fruit obvious in your life? Before we start looking at this topic in detail, I'd like to suggest a few points which I think would be worth bearing in mind.

First of all, you'll notice that the chapters are divided up under three headings – apart from the final chapter, these are 'The Father and…'; 'The Lord Jesus Christ and…'; and 'The Holy Spirit and…'. Each of these reflects the Christian understanding of the three-in-one God. We don't worship three separate gods, but the God of the Bible is a trinity – three persons – yet one God. Let me illustrate it this way: a triangle has three sides, yet is one shape. If you remove one of the sides, you no longer have a triangle. Similarly, God is three persons, yet he is one God. If you take away one of these, your view of God will be incomplete. We're going to look at how the fruit mentioned in Galatians describes the character of God the Father, was shown in the life of the Lord Jesus Christ, and is produced in Christian believers by the Holy Spirit. As this study focuses on the fruit of the Spirit, you'll find that the third section in each chapter is sometimes longer than the other two.

Secondly, the Bible teaches that when a person truly becomes a Christian believer, through repentance and faith in Jesus Christ, that person begins to have a living relationship with God. In John 15:1–8, Jesus uses the picture of a vine and its branches to illustrate the sort of relationship his followers have with him – he is the vine, we are the branches. As long as we remain in touch with Jesus, by loving him and obeying what he says, then we're in a position to receive the power of his Holy Spirit in much the same way as a branch receives nourishment from the vine. One way in which the Spirit shows his power in our lives is by producing in us the kind of spiritual fruit mentioned in Galatians 5:22,23.

Thirdly, and related to what's just been said, it is the fruit of the Spirit – he is the one who produces the fruit in our lives. Our responsibility is to co-operate with him by remaining in a loving, obedient relationship with the vine – Jesus Christ. We can't live a fruitful Christian life on our own – we are totally dependent on the Spirit's power at work in us.

Finally, it's interesting to note that Galatians 5:22,23 talks about the fruit – not fruits – of the Spirit. We can't pick and choose – we can't take joy and leave self-control, for example. The fruit of the Spirit comes as a package. It's like a vine laden with grapes – several grapes are produced, but it's still one fruit.

I'd be delighted if this study helped you to bear fruit for God. Don't be content with just answering the questions – let your study of this part of God's word motivate you to apply all that you learn to your everyday circumstances. Frequently read John 15:1–17 and look forward to a fruitful life!

How to use this study

Welcome to the 'Living out the life of Jesus' Bible study! My desire is that as you study and share your findings with others, you will be drawn into a closer relationship with the Lord.

This Bible study has two main emphases: the first is to encourage you to dig deep into the word of God because this is our main guide for living, and the second is to help you apply this word to your daily life. Only God's word is completely trustworthy and, if we are going to live in a way which will honour and please him, then we need to know what he says in the Bible. However, being merely familiar with what the Bible says is, in itself, insufficient. In order for God's word to be real and vital, there needs to be application of the truths that we read about there. The best way to do this is to co-operate with the Holy Spirit. Ask him to help you take on board what God is saying to you in the Bible. Ask him to apply his word to you so that there is no way that you can remain unchanged by its power. Biblical truth applied to our lives by the Holy Spirit results in spiritual growth and changed attitudes and behaviour.

This study is for either individual or group application. If you are sharing your answers with others in a group, this is a wonderful way to support and encourage one another. However, the most important part of the study is in preparation. Allow yourself plenty of time to read the questions and the Bible references. Get alone with the Lord and his word. Ask him for his help as you go through each of the questions. Don't concern yourself about 'wrong answers' – do as much as you can, as completely as you can. This is really your learning period. Fully prepared in this way, you will find that you will receive immense benefit from the subsequent sharing in your group. You will also be in a much stronger position to contribute thoughtfully and meaningfully – this will be greatly appreciated by both your leader and other group members.

The time taken in preparation will vary from person to person. Don't be concerned if it takes a while to complete each chapter. My intention is that the questions and Bible verses will cause you to linger in the Lord's presence. However, I suggest you avoid the temptation of answering all the questions from a chapter in one sitting the day or evening before you meet with the rest of your group to share what you have written. It might overwhelm you to tackle a whole chapter at a time. Instead, you'll probably find it helpful to divide up each chapter into study sections. For example, each one is already divided into three parts. Depending on the frequency with which your group meets, you might wish to do each section over two days, giving a six day preparation time, with about twenty minutes per day devoted to answering the questions, reading the Bible verses and praying about the application to your own life. This could be a suitable pattern if your group meets every week. On the other hand, if you meet with others every two weeks, you could complete the study by spending around twenty minutes every other day, or by spending less time each day but preparing your answers over a ten or twelve day period. The way you prepare is essentially up to you – different people have varying needs and responsibilities – but the important thing is that you develop a pattern of study which works for you and then stick to it! If you haven't approached Bible study in this way before, I'm sure you'll find that the discipline it involves will be extremely helpful in your everyday life.

May each of you display the fruit of the Spirit more and more as you work through this study, remembering to continually stay in touch with the Lord.

Notes for leaders

Leading a Bible study is a great privilege and responsibility. Not only do leaders need to thoroughly prepare the study material, but they also need to prepare themselves. This involves being in a close relationship with the Lord, arising out of personal Bible study and prayer, along with a commitment to live their lives to God's glory. No matter how much natural talent leaders might have, they are absolutely dependent upon the Lord for wisdom and help in leading their groups. My desire is that, as you study this material together with your group members, you will draw your strength from him and will become more like him.

Encourage your group members to write down their answers to the questions before coming to the Bible study meeting. In my own experience as group leader, and in talking with other leaders, I've found this to be a vital part of Christian growth. Preparation allows an opportunity to be guided by the Holy Spirit in answering the questions, whereas an 'off-the-cuff' response during the meeting, with no prayerful preparation time, is less likely to be helpful to others in the group. Asking that all members of your group prepare each chapter in advance of your meeting helps to encourage timid, less knowledgeable members to contribute their responses on a more equal footing with spiritually mature members – this, in turn, can lead to greater spiritual growth and unity within the group.

This Bible study will take about sixty to ninety minutes to discuss people's answers to the questions. It's important that all questions are covered in your meeting, because if you get into the habit of not discussing the final questions in each chapter, your members might not prepare answers to these questions for future chapters. I suggest, therefore, that you prepare a time schedule in advance of your meeting – write down your start time at the beginning, then the time you expect to complete the first section, and the second section, and finally the third section of the chapter to be discussed. In this way, you should be able to keep track of your time and know whether you need to slow down or speed up in discussing your group's responses.

May the Lord be constantly at your side as you seek to lead others into a deeper knowledge of him.

1| Love

'Love is patient and kind. Love is not jealous or boastful or proud or rude. Love does not demand its own way. Love is not irritable, and it keeps no record of when it has been wronged. It is never glad about injustice but rejoices whenever the truth wins out. Love never gives up, never loses faith, is always hopeful, and endures through every circumstance.'

1 Corinthians 13:4–7 (New Living Translation)

It is so easy to say, 'I love you,' and in most cases, those are powerful, healing words. The Scriptures warn us not to stop with lip service, but to show our love by our actions, our gifts, and our service. Instead of saying, 'Call me if there is anything I can do,' love says, 'I'm fixing dinner for your family tomorrow night. What time may I deliver it?' There is all the difference in the world between half-hearted offers and the robust delivery of a tangible gift.
Jan Silvious [1]

Pop and rock stars sing about it. Romantic novelists write about it. Pastors and ministers preach about it. In fact, we just can't live without it. Love. The very word conjures up all sorts of images – we talk about 'loving' a certain food, or 'loving' a husband or child. We also talk about 'loving' God. There is a saying that all is fair in love and war – an 'anything goes' mentality. While the phrase 'God is love' describes who he is essentially, this has been misused to mean that God ignores sin. In the middle of all these confusing impressions, how is the Christian to understand 'love'? It has been said that *'real love is not a feeling. It is an action, a commitment to appreciate and affirm others, to serve and sacrifice for them.'* [2] In this study, we will look at love as an attribute, or characteristic, of God the Father; love as a central element in the nature of the Lord Jesus Christ; and love as a work of the Holy Spirit, seen in the lives of Christians as the fruit of the Spirit.

The Father and love

There is tremendous relief in knowing that His love to me is utterly realistic, based at every point on prior knowledge of the worst about me, so that no discovery now can disillusion Him about me, in the way I am so often disillusioned about myself, and quench His determination to bless me.
J I Packer [3]

The Bible makes many references to love. Look up the following small selection of verses and write down what each says about God's love.

Read Psalm 103:13,17; Hosea 2:19; 1 John 4:9,10

Q The above verses give support to the idea that love is not only an emotion, but an action. In what way has your study of these verses altered or confirmed your ideas about what God's love is like?

Nowhere in all the world is love more clearly seen than on the cross of Calvary. Here we see the Father's love as he gives his dearly loved Son to be the Saviour for sinners, and the Son's love as he obeys the will of his Father. Ask the Lord to give you a fresh view of his love for you as you *take time* to think about the following four points about the cross:

◆ Here God's love is seen in action

◆ He secured the eternal salvation of all who believe

◆ His love is undeserved by us

◆ The cost to him was beyond measurement

Only one act of pure love, unsullied by any taint of ulterior motives, has ever been performed in the history of the world, namely the self-giving of God in Christ on the cross for undeserving sinners. That is why, if we are looking for a definition of love, we should look not in a dictionary, but at Calvary.
John R W Stott [4]

The Lord Jesus Christ and love

O the deep, deep love of Jesus!
Vast, unmeasured, boundless, free,
Rolling as a mighty ocean
In its fulness over me.
Underneath me, all around me,
Is the current of Thy love;
Leading onward, leading homeward,
To my glorious rest above.
Samuel Trevor Francis 5

1 John 4:8,16 tells us that God is love. Love is central to his very nature. It doesn't take a very intense reading of the New Testament to quickly notice that love motivated all Jesus' actions and relationships.

Read Mark 10:17–22; John 4:4–30; John 13:1–9

Q Look at the passages above and write down instances of love being shown by the Lord.

Q Choose one of the above passages and say what you learn from it about Jesus' love for you personally.

The Holy Spirit and love

Abiding in Christ is deciding to let Christ be our Source, surrender-
ing our life for His life, seeking His kingdom and His righteousness,
trusting Him to provide all that we need. It is choosing each day to
spend time with Him in His word and in conversation with Him. To
abide in Christ is to attach our delicate, fragile selves firmly and per-
manently into the Vine in order to receive His strength and security.
Cynthia Heald 6

While the Father is the source of love and Jesus is our example of what it means to love, the Holy Spirit produces love in the lives of Christians as they remain in fellowship with Christ. The King James Version of the Bible uses the term 'abiding in Christ' to describe this close relationship with the Lord.

As we remain in a close relationship with Christ, the Spirit produces in us:

Love for God

In Matthew 22:37, the Lord quotes from Deuteronomy 6:5. Both these verses tell us how we are to love God. What does it mean for you to love God in this way?

If we love God, how will it be shown in our lives? (See Psalm 97:10 and John 14:21.)

Love for other Christians

Many verses in the Bible emphasise how important it is to love other Christians. One of the clearest is John 13:34,35, where Jesus said: 'So now I am giving you a new commandment: Love each other. Just as I have loved you, you should love each other. Your love for one another will prove to the world that you are my disciples' (NLT). Look at the following imaginary sketches and, after choosing only one of them, answer the question: 'What practical steps would enable me to show the same kind of love to this person?'

◆ A woman in your church is widowed with two young children, aged nine and four. You see her in church every Sunday morning and recently you've noticed that she looks very tired and tense. She usually drives to church but lately you haven't seen her car in the church car park. You overheard her nine-year-old telling someone that he probably wouldn't be able to go away for a weekend next month with his Sunday School class as his mum had one or two things she needed to buy for his sister.

◆ A member of your Bible study group appears unusually distraught and emotional during one of your meetings, although she tries hard to keep this in check. When your Bible study finishes, you ask her if she would like to talk about what is obviously troubling her. She tells you that she is very anxious about her father who has been diagnosed with Alzheimer's disease and is going to require constant care. She works part-time and is at a loss to know what to do.

◆ Your minister/pastor is very busy in your congregation and has many responsibilities. You've received good Bible teaching from him and also encouragement when you were ill in hospital a couple of months ago. He has a large congregation to take care of and, although there are other people who are involved in various aspects of the church's ministry, you feel that he is in serious danger of becoming overloaded. You would like to show your appreciation to him.

◆ One of your friends has been a missionary overseas for several years and you've always looked forward to receiving his prayer letters. Recently, however, he has reported that his situation is becoming more and more difficult – he is severely understaffed at the hospital where he works; government officials are becoming increasingly hostile to the gospel; and his teenage daughter will soon be leaving her family to begin her secondary education at a boarding-school in the UK.

◆ He's a Christian, yet you find him *so* irritating. He's one of those 'sand-paper people' who cause friction and discomfort every time you make contact with them. You would rather just keep out of his way, but you've both been put together on the coffee-making rota after church. You don't want to complicate matters by asking for the rota to be changed – so you're going to have to see this one through. In fact, you're going to have to do more than just 'see it through' – you're going to have to love him.

Practical steps

If we cannot learn to love the Body of Christ, how will we ever be equipped to love our neighbours and the lost, let alone our enemies? So lift up! Build up! Exalt your brother and sister – at any cost.
Anne Meskey Elhajoui 7

If you had to translate these imaginary situations into real life, how would you get on? Are you willing to love another Christian you know in the way that Jesus loves you? Look around you – there's bound to be at least one who would welcome your love in action.

Love for those who are not Christians

> *The knowledge that God has loved me beyond all limits will compel me to go into the world to love others in the same way. I may get irritated because I have to live with an unusually difficult person. But just think how disagreeable I have been with God! Am I prepared to be identified so closely with the Lord Jesus that His life and His sweetness will be continually poured out through me? Neither natural love nor God's divine love will remain and grow in me unless it is nurtured. Love is spontaneous, but it has to be maintained through discipline.*
> Oswald Chambers 8

In Matthew 22:39, Jesus again quotes from the Old Testament, this time from Leviticus 19:18. In both these verses we are told to love our neighbour as ourselves. In Luke 10:29 an expert in religious law asked Jesus, 'Who is my neighbour?' In reply the Lord told the parable of the Good Samaritan – for the full story, see Luke 10:30–37. Using your imagination, translate this story into a twenty-first century environment. In doing this, consider the main principles of the parable and how they can be worked out in practice. Be as specific as you can.

With the Holy Spirit's help, how will you show the love of Jesus this week to someone who, as yet, is not a Christian? As you stay close to the Lord, trust him for this fruit in your life.

Personal comment

When I was a teenager, someone said to me that to understand 1 Corinthians 13:4–7, I should replace 'love' with my own name – 'Florence is patient and kind. Florence is not jealous ... Florence does not demand her own way ...' What a tall order! I think I was more discouraged after this advice than I was before it! I'm afraid I just didn't fit the bill. As I matured as a Christian, I began to realise that it is only as I surrender more and more to the Holy Spirit that he does the work and produces the fruit of love in my life. But what does it mean to surrender to the Holy Spirit? When we first become Christians, the Holy Spirit comes to live in us and it is easy to make the mistake of treating him like a visitor rather than a resident – he is allowed access to only one or two rooms in the house. We keep firmly shut the door to the messy, disorderly rooms which need a good clear out and clean up. We can't possibly let the Spirit into these rooms – he might want to change things! Surrendering to the Holy Spirit means I stop treating him as a guest in the house and realise that, when I became a Christian, I came under new management. He is not a guest but the owner! As the owner, he has the right to have access into all the rooms in the house, even those that no one else goes into. Am I prepared to allow the Spirit access to all areas of my life? Are there some areas that are still 'out of bounds' to him? Are there some rooms I still want to own and do things my way rather than his? Surrendering to the Holy Spirit in my life is not an overnight matter – it is an ongoing, lifelong process, where every day I need the Lord's forgiveness; I need strength to obey his Word; and I need to be willing to hand over the control of my life to him so that I can become the person he wants me to be.

As I remain in a close relationship with Jesus Christ, he helps me to be obedient to his will for me, and nourishes me in the same way as a branch receives nourishment from a vine. Look again at 1 Corinthians 13:4–7 – only the power of the Holy Spirit working in me can enable me to love like that. May the Lord help you and me to invite him into every area of our lives – only then will he produce the fruit of love in our lives.

2| Joy

'Always be full of joy in the Lord. I say it again – rejoice!'
Philippians 4:4 (NLT)

*Joy is the one thing most evident in those who have been caught by
the heavenly way and purpose of life. They have learned to live in
the strength and source of JOY Himself ... We are called to joy. It is
not optional but imperative that everyone who runs to win should
exhibit joy, the mark of maturity.*
De Vern F Fromke [1]

It was certainly a night to remember. Never before had a quiz show
contestant scooped the top prize of £1,000,000. The audience went wild
with delight. She went numb with shock, and then the tears started to
flow – not tears of sadness, she told the interviewer later, but tears of joy.
'This is the happiest day of my life!' she exclaimed. Were they really tears
of joy? Joy and happiness are often confused with each other. We all want
our fair share of happiness but, because being happy depends on our
circumstances, it is often short-lived. Joy, on the other hand, has been
defined as *'a deep sense of well-being that is not dependent upon favourable
circumstances, but rooted in a fundamental acceptance of, and confidence in,
the will of God.'* [2] However, this is not always our experience as Christians;
in this study, we will see that God experiences joy and that it's also a fruit
which the Holy Spirit produces in those who depend on Jesus Christ.

The Father and joy

If the Lord rejoices over us, we should rejoice in His service.
Matthew Henry [3]

There are several references in the Bible to God the Father showing joy or
delight. What do the following verses tell you about God's joy?

Read Psalm 104:31; Jeremiah 32:41; Zephaniah 3:17

Q Choose one of these verses and say why it particularly appeals to you.

Q Can you think of any situations when this verse might be especially helpful to you?

The Lord Jesus Christ and joy

What was the joy that Jesus had? Joy should not be confused with happiness. In fact, it is an insult to Jesus Christ to use the word 'happiness' in connection with Him. The joy of Jesus was His absolute self-surrender and self-sacrifice to His Father – the joy of doing that which the Father sent Him to do ... Jesus prayed that our joy might continue fulfilling itself until it becomes the same joy as His. Have I allowed Jesus Christ to introduce His joy to me?
Oswald Chambers 4

I find it very encouraging to read that Jesus knew joy. He came into the world to die, knowing that the cross lay ahead of him. He was under no misapprehensions regarding the circumstances of his life. Yet, he was no stranger to joy.

Read John 15:11; Hebrews 12:2; Psalm 45:7; Isaiah 53:3

Q Look at the verses above. What do they tell you about joy in the life of the Lord?

Q Jesus had a balance between joy and sorrow, and this is brought out in some Old Testament prophecies about him. Psalm 45:7 is one which talks about Jesus being filled with more joy than his companions. Another verse is Isaiah 53:3 where the Lord Jesus is described as being a man of sorrows who was familiar with suffering. How can these two verses be reconciled?

Q How do these aspects of the life of Jesus (joy and sorrow) encourage you in your present circumstances?

The Holy Spirit and joy

We do not have to search for God's joy; it is already our possession, waiting for us to choose it above lesser joys. Our inner experience may drift in and out of this joy, but always the joy is there, waiting for new opportunities to flood our whole being. It is ours to settle down in.
Warren and Ruth Myers [5]

The fruit of the Spirit is joy. As we remain close to the Lord, we're promised that we will experience the fruit of joy (John 15:9–11). Joy of believers isn't restricted to the New Testament, however. Note the following Old Testament references and describe in your own words the significance of the joy which each verse talks about.

Read Nehemiah 8:10; Isaiah 12:3; Isaiah 35:10

There are at least 19 references to joy in the Psalms alone.

Read Psalm 5:11; 16:11; 30:5; 43:4; 126:5; 132:9

Using the psalms above, take time now to reflect on what each verse has to say to you about joy in your experience.

Give thanks to God for the joy which *is yours* as a believer in the Lord.

Joy in the New Testament

There are several verses throughout the New Testament which talk about joy. One New Testament book which frequently mentions joy is Philippians – in fact, joy is mentioned in every chapter of this book but with a different emphasis each time. In chapter 1, Paul writes from prison in Rome about joy in suffering; in chapter 2, about joy in serving; in chapter 3, about joy in believing; and in chapter 4, about joy in giving.

At your leisure, read through the book of Philippians, noting the verses which talk about the Christian's joy. *Take time* to think about how you can apply them to your own circumstances.

Hindrances to joy

Don't let sin, neglect of the Bible, and prayerlessness rob you of your joy. God wants you to have joy ... Joy lubricates the machinery of life and makes everything run much smoother. A joyful Christian is a strong Christian: Satan has a harder time tempting the man who has joy in his heart. A joyful Christian is a witnessing Christian because he has something exciting to share with others, and they can see the difference.
Warren W Wiersbe 6

Although the Holy Spirit produces joy in our lives, we're not always conscious of this joy as we go about our daily work and responsibilities. Our vision of God can be obscured and, as a result, our joy in him gets less. Look at the following verses and identify, in each case, *the reason* for the lack of joy and *what was done* to restore it.

Problem	Response/Effect
Psalm 32:3,4	Psalm 32:5/Psalm 51:12
Psalm 107:11	Jeremiah 15:16
James 4:2	John 16:24

Are any of these reasons – sin, neglect of the Bible, prayerlessness – responsible for lack of joy in your life? If so, you might find it helpful to write down what the specific joy-stealer is, along with ways in which you can deal with it. For example, if you've been neglecting reading the Bible, you could make a definite commitment to set aside specific times each day when you will make Bible reading a priority. Sometimes you'll need to mark a definite time on your calendar or diary and view it as an unbreakable appointment with the Lord. It could mean having to get out of bed earlier, or using part of your lunch break, or missing a television programme. The time might vary from one day to another – that's okay, as long as you carve out some time each day to learn from God's Word. Use the space below to write down the particular joy-stealer in your life at present, along with how you plan to deal with it.

Joy in difficulties

The joy of encountering hardship springs from the knowledge that God is at work in our lives to make us more like Him. It is our choice to trust God with our lives so that steadfastness under pressure enables us to mature in Christ, fully prepared to be useful to the Lord.
Cynthia Heald [7]

The Holy Spirit produces the fruit of joy in us as we trust in Jesus, but this is no guarantee that life will always go smoothly – when Christians go through difficulties, joy is still a fruit of the Spirit, even in hard circumstances.

Read Acts 5:41; 2 Corinthians 6:10; James 1:2–4

Write down ways in which these verses are an encouragement to you.

What difficulties are in your life right now? Are you consistently bringing them to the Lord in prayer? Like King Hezekiah (2 Kings 19:14), spread them in front of God, asking him to show you how you can best respond. Be completely honest with the Lord as you look for his help to resolve the situation and allow him to restore your joy once again.

Personal comment

You may have heard of the (true) story about a little girl whose parents belonged to a very strict religious denomination. While out walking one day, the child saw a donkey looking over a fence. She ran up to the donkey and, stroking its head, she said to her mother, 'Mummy, this must be a Christian donkey because he has such a long face!' Although this did produce some wry laughter from my family when I read it out, it really is such a caricature of what it means to be a Christian! There's no place in our Christian experience for long, sullen faces! In this study, we've learned that joy is not the same as happiness; it's something far deeper. The Christian isn't always smiling, but there is joy within us which is deep and lasting, no matter what the circumstances. In order for this to be the case, our joy has to be in a source which doesn't change – that source is God himself. As I trust in the Lord Jesus Christ, the Holy Spirit produces in my life the fruit of joy: joy from knowing that all my sins are forgiven – gone, never to return and trouble me; and joy because I have a Lord who is completely trustworthy. I can experience joy even if I might not be particularly happy with my present circumstances because I know that God controls all the details of my life for his own purpose and glory (Romans 8: 28–30). I can be joyful because he has promised that he will never leave me nor forsake me. I know joy because Jesus said that he was going to prepare accommodation suitable for me in heaven, and I have his promise that he will welcome his faithful servants to that heaven by saying 'Enter in to the joy of your Lord' (Matthew 25:21, NKJV).

Habakkuk 3:17–19 gives us a picture of a believer whose confidence in God causes him to rejoice – even when the bottom falls out of his world and a lot of things just don't seem to make any sense. To what extent could our prize-winning contestant echo Habakkuk's words? To what extent can you echo his words? As we remain in a close relationship with Jesus, the Holy Spirit can produce a harvest of joy in our lives – regardless of our circumstances. Will you allow him to do this?

3| **Peace**

'You will keep in perfect peace all who trust in you, whose thoughts are fixed on you!'
Isaiah 26:3 (NLT)

The Scriptures are laden with promises that, as we have the grace to believe, will build peace into the core of our being. This does not mean that life will always be easy. On the contrary, life is often filled with physical pain, emotional turmoil, spiritual upheaval. So we must understand peace not as an elimination of troubling circumstances, but as an assurance and trust in God in spite of our circumstances ... as we grow in the grace and knowledge of our Lord Jesus Christ, the fruit of the Spirit increasingly can be ours.
Max Anders [1]

How would you define 'peace'? It's certainly something which is in great demand – politicians want peace, or absence of war, for their countries; business leaders look for peace, or harmony, among their employees; stressed-out parents are desperate for peace, or quietness, at the end of a busy day; and each of us, if we're honest, longs for peace, or inner calm and tranquillity, to be a lasting feature of our lives. One author suggests that *'peace is the absence of anxiety and the presence of trusting assurance in the promises of God.'* [2] In this study, we'll look at the source of peace and how we can experience this God-given quality, as we depend on Christ, and are directed and empowered by the Holy Spirit.

The Father and peace

God, who loves peace, makes peace, and breathes peace, will be with us. 'Peace be with you' is a sweet benediction; but for the God of peace to be with us is far more. Thus we have the fountain as well as

the streams, the sun as well as his beams. If the God of peace be with us, we shall enjoy the peace of God which passeth all understanding, even though outward circumstances should threaten to disturb. If men quarrel, we shall be sure to be peace-makers, if the Maker of peace be with us.
Charles Spurgeon 3

God knows what it is to be at peace, both with himself and with Christian believers. What do the following verses tell you about the relationship between God and peace?

Read Numbers 6:24–26; 1 Kings 2:33; Hebrews 13:20,21

Q From the above references, choose one which particularly impressed you. How has this helped you gain a better understanding of the relationship between God the Father and peace?

Q In addition to Hebrews 13:20,21, there are several other verses which speak about the 'God of peace.' In what way can this description of God give you comfort and encouragement in your present circumstances?

The Lord Jesus Christ and peace

God's mark of approval, whenever you obey him, is peace. He sends an immeasurable, deep peace; not a natural peace, 'as the world gives,' but the peace of Jesus. Whenever peace does not come, wait until it does, or seek to find out why it is not coming. If you are acting on your own impulse, or out of a sense of the heroic, to be seen by others, the peace of Jesus will not exhibit itself.
Oswald Chambers 4

One of the titles given in Isaiah 9:6 to the promised Messiah is 'Prince of Peace'. In Luke 2:14, when the angels proclaim the birth of the Lord Jesus Christ to the shepherds, they talk about peace on earth. However, in Matthew 10:34 and Luke 12:51, Jesus says that he didn't come to bring peace to the earth. How do you understand this apparent contradiction? (Your thoughts about this might help you to answer someone who is confused about why there is such an absence of peace in the world.)

In the Jewish culture when Jesus was on earth, the peace greeting, or *Shalom*, was commonly practised and Jesus used it himself (Luke 24:36; John 20:19,21,26). Extending peace or desiring the welfare of another person was something that was valued in everyday relationships.

Read John 14:27

Q What is the peace that Jesus gives?

Q In what way(s) is it different from other kinds of peace?

Q In what way(s) can this verse encourage you at the present time?

The Holy Spirit and peace

For us, peace with God is not simply an armistice; it is a war ended forever; and now the redeemed hearts of former enemies of the cross are garrisoned with a peace that transcends all human knowledge

and outsoars any wings of flight we can possibly imagine.
Billy Graham [5]

In order to know peace, the kind that is supernatural and lasting, we have to know the God of peace. So, before we can have the peace *of* God, we need to have peace *with* God.

The upward dimension – peace with God

Peace with God is not the same as feeling at peace with ourselves or with the world in general. To be at peace with God means that he is at peace with us – the hostility which previously existed between us and God was removed when we believed that Jesus died on the cross as the sacrifice for our sins. Look at the verses below and write down what they tell us about having peace with God.

Read Romans 5:1; Colossians 1:19,20

The inward dimension – peace of God

Many Bible verses make it clear that peace which is genuine and lasting comes from God and is given to us by the Holy Spirit. The wonderful news is that this peace is available to all who have peace with God! The following verses speak very clearly and directly about this peace. In your own words, describe the main message of each verse.

Read Psalm 4:8; Isaiah 26:3; Colossians 3:15

Choose one of the above verses that has been meaningful to you in your experience.

We often need to be concerned about people or circumstances in our lives, but the Bible warns us about allowing a legitimate concern to become a worry or an anxiety which will overwhelm us and disturb our peace. Read the verses in the following table and write down what we shouldn't be anxious about. Why do we not need to be anxious?

Verses	Don't be anxious about...
Matthew 6:25	
Matthew 6:28	
Matthew 6:31	
Matthew 6:34	
Matthew 10:19	
Philippians 4:6	

Try committing one of the above verses to memory and act on it the next time anxiety threatens to disturb your peace.

> *When you look over what it was you worried about this time last week, did it happen? Was it worth the worry? If it was – if the worst thing that you could imagine actually did happen – where did the worry get you?*
> Elisabeth Elliot [6]

Rest and peace often go together. In Mark 6:31, Jesus instructed his disciples to go *with him* to get some rest. This illustrates the importance of staying close to Christ – apart from him, there is no rest and no peace.

How often do you follow the instruction in Mark 6:31? If this is an area you've been neglecting, are you prepared to remedy this with the Holy Spirit's help?

> *Jesus lived a life of unbroken fellowship with His Father. It was His constant connectedness to God that enabled Him to have peace in the midst of turmoil. If I abide in Christ, I, too, can experience peace in the midst of chaos. But I must stay connected to my Lord, as Jesus stayed connected to His Father.*
> Lorraine Pintus [7]

The outward dimension – peace towards others

Although the Holy Spirit produces the fruit of peace in our lives when we're at peace with God and are daily living close to Jesus, this peace is not only for our own personal benefit. Many verses in the Bible emphasise the importance of extending peace to others. Look at the following passages and note what each has to say about peace in our relationships.

Read Matthew 5:9; 2 Corinthians 13:11; Ephesians 4:3

Q Some of these verses refer specifically to peace with other Christians. Why is it important to maintain this peace?

Read Romans 12:18

Q Some things are beyond our ability to control, and peace with others will not always depend on us. How do you suggest we might behave in such situations?

External peace doesn't always depend upon us. We should always seek to be peace-makers (see Matthew 5:9), but our sense of self-worth cannot be based on an external world that we may or may not be able to control.
Neil Anderson 8

Personal comment

We've seen in this study that, as Christians, we have peace with God. As we remain in a close relationship with the Lord, we experience the peace of God. However, if I'm honest, I don't always feel at peace in my own mind. If I've sinned in a particular area, the Holy Spirit's peace will seem far away and, in order to know his peace once again, I must confess that specific sin to God, and ask for his forgiveness. At other times, though, it might not be any particular sin which is robbing me of my peace, but the presence of anxious thoughts. If allowed to take root, they can destroy my inner calm and tranquillity. I've found the following to be helpful.

Firstly, anxiety and peace are mutually exclusive – if we're anxious, we don't feel at peace, but if we experience the peace of God, anxiety can't get a foothold. The two can't exist together at the same time. It's useful to be familiar with Bible passages which illustrate God's desire for us to know his peace. A helpful verse is 2 Corinthians 10:5b which says '…we take captive every thought to make it obedient to Christ' (NIV). Don't let anxious thoughts have free reign in your mind. Take hold of the thought – capture it – and place it under the control of the Lord. Do this consciously, through prayer, asking for the Holy Spirit's help so that you can place your thoughts in submission to Christ's authority in your life. Read again Matthew 6:25–34. Then look at verse 33, which focuses our minds on God and his kingdom. I like what the New Living Translation says: 'He will give you all you need from day to day if you live for him and make the kingdom of God your primary concern.' What a great recipe for peace and for defeating anxiety and worry!

Secondly, learn to accept what you can't change. The old prayer which says: 'God grant me the serenity to accept the things I cannot change, courage to change the things I can and wisdom to know the difference' is not far wrong.

Thirdly, move your focus away from yourself – make an encouraging phone call to a friend; listen to what other people are saying; focus on God. I just love the verse quoted at the very beginning of this study from Isaiah 26:3: 'Fix your thoughts on God and he will keep you in perfect peace!'

4| Patience

'......let us lay aside every weight, and the sin which doth so easily beset us, and let us run with patience the race which is set before us.'
Hebrews 12:1 (KJV)

Patience is the transcendent radiance of a loving and tender heart which, in its dealings with those around it, looks kindly and graciously upon them. Patience graciously, compassionately and with understanding judges the faults of others without unjust criticism. Patience also includes perseverance – the ability to bear up under weariness, strain and persecution when doing the work of the Lord.
Billy Graham 1

Have you ever stood in front of your microwave oven as it heats a bowl of soup and found yourself telling it to hurry up? Can we really not wait patiently for even a couple of minutes? The Bible has a few things to tell us about patience and, depending on which translation you're reading, you might come across words like 'endurance', 'perseverance', 'long-suffering', and 'standing firm'. These all suggest that patience involves active, concentrated effort in the face of difficulties or provocations. Patience may also include waiting. This means realising that our timing may not be God's timing. Here's a definition of patience which I particularly like: *'Patience is accepting a difficult situation from God without giving Him a timetable to remove it.'* 2 In this study, we'll look at patience as a characteristic of God the Father; how it is demonstrated in the life of the Lord Jesus Christ; and as a further aspect of the fruit of the Holy Spirit.

The Father and patience

Our God is patient and long-suffering. He is never in a hurry, and He is seldom on our time schedule! Yet He is our Father, who is continually working all things together for our good. And so He tells us to rest – to be calm and peaceful; and to wait – to anticipate, to count upon, to watch for Him. A good way to respond to the complexities of life!
Cynthia Heald [3]

Although relatively few verses in the Bible speak *specifically* about the patience of God, the theme of his patience in dealing with human beings throughout the course of history runs right through the whole book. How wonderful to know that God is patient! One example of God's patience can be seen in the way he dealt with the initially disobedient Jonah, as well as with the city of Nineveh. In Jonah 1:1–3, God gives Jonah a command which he disobeys. In Jonah 3:1–3, the prophet is again given the same command to go to Nineveh to proclaim God's message – this time Jonah obeys.

Read Jonah 1–3

Q What examples of God's patience can you detect from your reading of the events which took place between Jonah receiving his first and his second commands? In what way(s) does this speak to you personally?

Q Nineveh was the capital city of Assyria – a great empire, but desperately wicked and the most feared enemy of Israel at the time. In Jonah 3:5–10, we read of the repentance of the Ninevites and the mercy and compassion of God towards them. How is this an example of God's patience?

Q In what way(s) can this give you hope and encouragement for the town or city in which you're living at the present time? (See also 2 Peter 3:9,15.)

Q How do these references to God's patience encourage you?

The Lord Jesus Christ and patience

I praise and glorify Thee, O Blessed Jesus, for Thy invincible patience on the Cross Thou hadst assumed; from which no reproaches, no enticing promises would induce Thee to come down. No, not for one short moment wouldest Thou leave that, which Thou hadst ascended of Thine own free will.
Thomas à Kempis 4

'Love is patient...' – so reads part of 1 Corinthians 13:4. We've already seen in an earlier chapter that love is central to the character of the Lord Jesus Christ. It should be no surprise to us, then, that he is also patient. In Luke 2:41–52, we read of the twelve-year-old Jesus at the temple when he went to Jerusalem with his parents for the Feast of the Passover. The next time we read of Jesus is eighteen years later when he is baptized by John at the start of his public ministry. How necessary do you think patience was in the Lord's experience during these years from age twelve to thirty?

The patience of Jesus can be seen in his many dealings with people throughout his earthly life and this comes to an amazing climax as he hangs on the cross, dying.

Read one of the following: Matthew 27:32–50; Mark 15:21–37; Luke 23:26–46; John 19:17–30

Q Record in what way(s) the Lord showed patient endurance throughout the whole horrific episode.

The Lord's patience, however, is not all-encompassing – he doesn't tolerate every kind of attitude and behaviour just because patience is one of his characteristics.

Read Matthew 23:13–32; Luke 9:41; John 2:13–16

Q Write down what the Lord is not patient with.

Q Which one of the above passages makes the greatest impression upon you? Share with your group the reasons for your answer.

The Holy Spirit and patience

The fortitude and patience of Job, though not small, gave way in his severe troubles; but his faith was fixed upon the coming of his Redeemer, and this gave him a stedfastness and constancy, though every other dependence, particularly the pride and boast of a self-righteous spirit, was tried and consumed.
Matthew Henry [5]

The Bible gives us several examples of people who displayed patience of an extraordinary kind – patience that came from God. I've selected two of these people, one from the Old Testament and one from the New Testament. The Old Testament character is Job and he is an example of one who suffered long – he endured appalling events in his life, yet James 5:10,11 specifically mentions him as one who persevered. The New Testament character is Simeon and he is an example of one who waited expectantly for God to fulfil his promise that he would see the Messiah. Both men exercised patience, but in very different circumstances.

Read Job 1,2

Q Make a list of the things which Job endured.

Q Which verses suggest patience on Job's part?

Q Does this alter your understanding of what it means to be patient? If so, in what way? If not, why not?

Read Job 13:15; 19:25–27; Luke 2:25–35

Q How might these statements from a greatly afflicted believer encourage you, or someone you know, at the present time?

Q We meet Simeon in Luke 2:25–35. In what way(s) did he show patience? How does this differ from the patience shown by Job?

Q What evidence is there from these verses that Simeon was living close to God?

Q Why is this important if we are to show the fruit of patience in our lives?

Patience is something which doesn't come naturally to most of us. We can perhaps exercise some degree of patience as long as our own resources aren't stretched for too long. But when a distressing situation continues, with little hope of improvement, we start to crack. At times like this, the Word of God comes to us again and we hear the Lord reminding us to stay close to him (John 15). Our own natural patience is so inadequate in helping us to cope well, but the Holy Spirit produces this fruit in those who remain vitally connected to Jesus.

The following are some examples of when you might need to exercise patience – feel free to add some of your own as well!

◆ When you have difficulties in your life. James 1:3 says that 'the testing of your faith develops perseverance'. What reason is given in verse 4 for the importance of perseverance? From your own life or someone else's, give an example of perseverance in action.

◆ When you suffer persecution. The New Living Translation says '... if you suffer for doing right and are patient beneath the blows, God is pleased with you' (1 Peter 2:20b). List three ways in which Christians in our culture today might 'suffer for doing right'.

If you're currently going through a time of persecution because you're doing what is right, *take time now* to reflect on this verse and be encouraged that the Lord is pleased with you. Thank him for this.

◆ When you're waiting for God to make his will known to you (Isaiah 40:31). Below are some imaginary situations. Choose one of these and say how you might counsel or encourage the people concerned.

– John was made redundant three months ago and, despite having several interviews, no one has yet offered him a job.

– Julie is 35 and single, and would love to meet and marry 'Mr Right'.

– The Smiths are convinced that the Lord wants to move them to another part of the country, but their house has been on the market for eight months, with very little interest from potential buyers.

– Sandra and Mark have been attending a clinic for infertile couples for several months and there's no guarantee that their treatment will be successful.

- Paul has graduated with a good honours degree and has several career options open to him. He's very keen to follow the path that God has for him, but he doesn't yet know what that is.

- How patient are you in waiting for God's guidance in your life? Remember that patience is a fruit of the Spirit and isn't something you can manufacture. Ask the Lord to produce this fruit in you as you submit your circumstances to his direction and control.

◆ When you live each day for the Lord. Look carefully at Hebrews 12:1. What hinders you as you run towards your eternal goal? What is the sin that so easily entangles you? *Take time now* to consider this and to confess it to the Lord, who is so ready and willing to put you back in the race of life and welcome you at the finishing line.

[The] grace of patience – which is either the meek endurance of ill because it is of God, or the calm waiting for promised good till his time to dispense it comes – (is) the full persuasion that such trials are divinely appointed, are the needed discipline of God's children, are but for a definite period, and are not sent without abundant promises of 'songs in the night'.
Robert Jamieson *et al* [6]

Personal comment

Have you praised God recently for his patience? Are you encouraged by the patience shown by Jesus? Did the examples of patience in the lives of Job and Simeon help you to gain a better understanding of what the word actually means? While writing this study, I was greatly struck by the different ways in which patience can be worked out in practice. On the one hand, there is the 'tough' side of patience – persevering, enduring, 'hanging in there', when things are incredibly difficult and distressing; on the other hand, there is the 'quiet' side of patience – waiting, trustingly and expectantly, until God's will for my life is clarified in his own timing. In some situations, both of these seem to merge together, so it isn't always easy to separate the two. I love Hebrews 12:1–4 which encouraged me to run with patience the race that God has set before me. When I was at school, I enjoyed athletics, particularly running the 100 metre and 200 metre races. In the 200 metre race I was often conscious of other competitors as we turned the curve in the track. At these times, I had to focus my attention on what was ahead – the finishing tape – and not allow anything else to distract me. Even when my goal wasn't in sight – I couldn't see the finishing tape from all points of the track – I knew it was there and that was what I was aiming for. I can run God's race with patience only as I focus on Jesus and not on myself or what is going on around me. To do this, I must remain close to him and draw my energy from being connected to him through a living and vital relationship. Over the next few days, prepare to strip down and tone up, as you seek, with the Holy Spirit's help, to run with patience the race that is set before you. Why not begin to spend five extra minutes in prayer or reading the Bible?

5 | Kindness

'Therefore, as God's chosen people, holy and dearly loved, clothe yourselves with compassion, kindness, humility, gentleness and patience.'
Colossians 3:12

Biblically appraised, kindness is far more than just being nice or polite. It is a view of people – regardless of whether they're rich, smart, or attractive – that leads to intentional action on their behalf. It is nothing less than deliberately imitating the kindness we've been shown by God.
Cole Huffman [1]

Are you known by your friends and family as a kind person? Does your kindness (or lack of it) make a real difference in your home, church or workplace? Kindness is something that people notice. Just a day or two after our family had moved house to a different part of the country, someone from the local church arrived at the door with a pot of homemade jam. She introduced herself to my husband and me and said she wanted to welcome us to the city. This small gesture showed us that at least one person cared at a time when we were finding it difficult to settle in to our new surroundings. How much we appreciated her kindness! One author claims that *'kindness is treating others well in word and deed.'* [2] The Bible contains many references to the kindness of God and the Lord Jesus Christ, and it is the Spirit's desire to produce the fruit of kindness in the lives of all Christians. Some Bible translations use the word 'gentleness'. The original Greek word implies the idea of useful or appropriate kindness, involving a sensitivity to others.

The Father and kindness

We all like to be treated kindly. How good it is, then, for us to know that God is kind.

Read Isaiah 54:8; Romans 2:4; Titus 3:3–7

Q Write down what you learn about the kindness of God in the verses above.

Q In Romans 11:22, we read of 'the kindness and sternness of God'. How does this help you to understand more of God's character?

'You didn't think, did you, that just by pointing your finger at others you would distract God from seeing all your misdoings and from coming down on you hard? Or did you think that because he's such a nice God, he'd let you off the hook? Better think this one through from the beginning. God is kind, but he's not soft. In kindness he takes us firmly by the hand and leads us into a radical life change.'
Romans 2:3,4 *The Message* [3]

Q How about sharing with your group specific ways in which you have experienced God's kindness in your life?

While your answers to the above questions are still fresh in your mind, *take time* to thank God for his kindness to you personally.

The Lord Jesus Christ and kindness

Women adored Jesus Christ during His life on earth. No man ever showed the caring concern for their well-being as He did. Jesus raised their dead. He healed their diseases and commanded tormenting demons to depart from them. And He treasured their presence and companionship.
Helene Ashker [4]

Read Matthew 12:17–21

Q This passage quotes a prophecy from the Old Testament about Jesus. Which of these verses speak of his kindness?

Q In what way(s) are you encouraged by this?

The Lord was immensely kind in his dealings with people. Women particularly appreciated this as they belonged to a society which treated them as second-class citizens. Jesus, however, valued women as much as men and included them as his friends.

Read Matthew 9:20–22, (see also fuller account in Luke 8:43–48); Luke 7:11–15; John 4:4–29; John 8:3–11

Q Write down what each incident tells you about the Lord's kindness towards women.

Jesus' kindness did not stop even when he was suffering and dying.

Read John 19:25–27

Q What can you learn from this passage?

The Holy Spirit and kindness

...if you are absorbed in your own life and your own problems, then no matter how nice you are, you really are not kind to other people. You can be sweet, but not helpful... Kindness is active interest in

others, not just a passing hello. Kindness is going out of your way to come alongside or to lend a hand to someone who needs you. If you are absorbed with yourself, you will never see that others are in need too.
Jan Silvious 5

The Holy Spirit produces the fruit of kindness in the lives of those who rely on the Lord. He does this by drawing their focus away from themselves and onto others. Not all people who show kindness to others are Christians, but all Christians should certainly be showing some evidence of kindness! All who claim to be believers in the Lord are enabled to show kindness by the power of the Holy Spirit living in them. Kindness is very much an outward aspect of the fruit of the Spirit. Although far from perfect, King David was described as 'a man after God's own heart' (I Samuel 13:14). 2 Samuel 9:1–13 gives an account of David desiring to show kindness like God's kindness.

Read 2 Samuel 9:1–13

Q Write down (a) who David was being kind to; (b) why he was being kind; (c) what happened as a result of his kindness.

As you go through this week, ask the Lord to show you areas in your life where you are not being kind and ask him to help you to demonstrate this fruit on a regular basis.

Several Bible verses encourage us to be kind towards others. Look up the verses below and match them up with the appropriate examples of kindness.

Verses	Examples of kindness
Matthew 10:42	Doing good to others
Hebrews 13:16	Gentle instruction
Hebrews 13:2	Cup of cold water
2 Timothy 2:24,25	Hospitality

Q From these verses, choose one which particularly challenges you and give a reason for your choice.

There is a very thought-provoking passage recorded for us in Matthew 25:31–46. Jesus is looking ahead to the final judgement, where true believers will be separated from false believers/unbelievers. The Lord is *not* teaching that we can earn salvation by being kind to others – this would be completely contrary to other Bible verses, eg Ephesians 2:8,9. However, he is emphasising the importance of Christians being active as a result of their faith. The actions mentioned in this passage don't turn someone into a Christian, but they are examples of how Christians should behave towards those in need.

Six ways of showing kindness

◆ Food for the hungry

◆ Drink for the thirsty

◆ Hospitality for the stranger

◆ Clothes for the naked

◆ Care for the sick

◆ Visit for the prisoner

Read Matthew 25:31–46

Q List specific ways in which you could show ongoing kindness to the kinds of people identified in this passage.

Remember that you are doing this in obedience to the Lord and with the help of his Spirit, and not primarily because you are a naturally kind and sympathetic person. This is the difference between the fruit of the Spirit and the fruit of natural concern for these people. As you live close to the Lord and allow his Spirit to work in your life, he will help you to be kind – even in your most difficult relationships!

Does the Matthew 25 passage challenge you about your attitude and behaviour towards others? As you think deeply about this question, ask the Lord to help you to be obedient to what he wants you to do.

> *We need to be concerned. We need to have compassion. This is not the same as telling others of the Gospel. Opportunities to help others allow us to show genuine love, to earn the right to be heard, so that we can tell them about Jesus Christ.*
> Ruth Bell Graham 6

Read 1 Thessalonians 5:15

The second part of this passage says, '... always try to be kind to each other and to everyone else'. In our efforts to show kindness to Matthew 25 people, let's not forget to show kindness to those in our church fellowship. Below are some suggestions you might wish to take on board. Choose one or more to act on this week (or add some ideas of your own).

Showing kindness

◆ Send an encouraging card or letter to someone who is ill

◆ Give a dinner invitation to students living away from home

◆ Take an elderly person to lunch

◆ Babysit for a single parent so that s/he can have an evening out

◆ Take a gift to someone who has just moved into new accommodation

◆ Pay a visit to someone confined to home

◆ Buy a book that you have found helpful to give to a new Christian

> *Amid the pressures of today, the increasing global turmoil ... we who are Christians must be alert to the needs of others. Is there a letter that we could write? A simple deed of kindness that we should do? An encouraging word to give to someone who is desperate to hear? Time that we ought to take to listen? Is there someone we should invite for a meal or a cup of tea?*
> Ruth Bell Graham 7

Personal comment

Have you bought any new clothes lately? How much thought did you give to the colour, style, fabric? Clothes that suit us improve our appearance and our confidence, don't they? We like to look good and to dress as well as we can afford. The Bible gives us some advice on dressing well – in Colossians 3:12, Christians are to put on 'compassion, kindness, humility, gentleness and patience'. How well do these 'clothes' fit you? How much work does the Holy Spirit have to do in your life before they are a perfect fit? In the last study, on patience, we considered the verse from Hebrews 12:1 which talks about throwing off those things which hinder us or hold us back in our Christian lives. While we throw some things off, let's not forget to put other things on! Colossians 3:12 is one example of what we can put on, and included in the list is kindness.

Although we must always be ready to tell others about our Christian faith, actions sometimes speak louder than words. Have you heard of a form of outreach that some churches practise which is known as 'servant evangelism'? Members offer free services such as window cleaning, lawn mowing, car washing, exam tutoring etc, just to show to the community that God is kind. Once people realise that there are no strings attached, some have become more open to what the Christians have to say about what God has done in their lives.

Are your clothes of kindness in good shape or have they become stretched as a result of reaching out to difficult people? Have they become a bit dirty or drab? Have they started to become threadbare? If your answer is 'yes', think again about your relationship to the Lord Jesus Christ. Re-read John 15:1–17 to remind yourself that he is the Vine and you are a branch receiving nourishment directly from him. Don't focus primarily on the production of fruit, but on the Lord himself. Thinking about his kindness should make you want to be like him and show kindness to others. Don't be caught running naked! Make sure that you are wearing the Colossians 3:12 wardrobe – clothes which have been made by the Master Tailor himself.

6| Goodness

'For you were once darkness, but now you are light in the Lord. Live as children of light (for the fruit of the light consists in all goodness, righteousness and truth) and find out what pleases the Lord.'

Ephesians 5:8–10

God is good. He is the source of whatever is true, noble, right, pure, lovely, admirable, excellent, or praiseworthy. We judge goodness with Him as the standard.

James Aderman [1]

What sort of things come into your mind when you hear the word 'goodness'? The Bible tells us that God is good. In fact, he is infinitely good – he cannot be more good than he already is – and he is consistently good – there is never a time when goodness is not part of his character. In defining 'good', the Life Application Study Bible uses the terms *'kind, profitable, excellent, fitting, or appropriate.'* [2] It also defines 'good' as being *'morally right'*. No human being is naturally good but, as Christians, the Holy Spirit works to produce the fruit of goodness in us – he wants to reflect in our lives this aspect of the character of God. As we consider goodness as part of the nature of God, which is shown in the life of Jesus, we'll also see how this fruit can be seen in us if we consistently allow the Holy Spirit to influence our lives.

The Father and goodness

How good is the God we adore,
Our faithful, unchangeable Friend!
His love is as great as His power,
And knows neither measure nor end!

Joseph Hart [3]

One of the greatest acknowledgements of God's goodness can be found in Psalm 107. In some versions of the Bible, the term is 'unfailing love'.

Read Psalm 107

Q Identify four different types of people to whom God extends his goodness. To help you, the first can be found in verses 4–9; the second in 10–16; the third in 17–20; and the fourth in 23–30.

Q What does this tell you about God's goodness, and how does it encourage you?

The Lord Jesus Christ and goodness

…Grace always comes by Jesus Christ. The law was given by Moses, but grace came by Jesus Christ. This does not mean that before Jesus was born of Mary there was no grace. God dealt in grace with mankind, looking forward to the incarnation and death of Jesus before Christ came. Now, since He's come and gone to the Father's right hand, God looks back upon the cross as we look back upon the cross. [Every believer] from Abel on was saved by looking forward to the cross. Grace came by Jesus Christ. And everybody that's been saved since the cross is saved by looking back at the cross.
A W Tozer [4]

There are at least three ways in which Jesus displayed the goodness of God – these are his perfection, his mercy, and his grace.

One area in which Jesus demonstrated his perfect nature was in his response to temptation. Both Matthew and Luke record one period when he was tempted by the devil.

Read Luke 4:1–13

Q Describe in your own words the three different temptations that are highlighted here.

Q Why was it vitally important that Jesus did not give in to Satan's temptations?

Can you identify temptations in your life which you are finding difficult to resist? Being tempted is not a sin but focusing on the temptation by thinking about it and giving in to it *is* displeasing to God and is, therefore, sinful. Bring the matter to the Lord – he understands (see Hebrews 4:15) and will provide an escape route for you (see 1 Corinthians 10:13). If possible, identify *in advance* the specific way of escape from your temptation and take it before you find yourself giving in to it.

The second aspect of the Lord's goodness can be seen by considering his *mercy*. Mercy can mean forgiving someone who doesn't deserve to be forgiven. It can also involve showing pity and compassion towards those in need. The following two passages give examples of Jesus' compassion.

Read Matthew 9:36–38; Mark 6:34,37a

Q Write down the instructions Jesus gave to his disciples.

Q What does this tell you about the responsibility of Jesus' followers today?

Our compassion is sometimes only in our minds – it doesn't move us to action. Think of a person known to you to whom you could show mercy by being actively compassionate. Write down specific ways in which you could do this and then ask the Lord for his help in carrying this out.

In several parts of the New Testament, we read about the *grace* of the Lord Jesus Christ. This is a third way in which he demonstrates his goodness. Grace can be seen as *'God's inexplicable kindness; unconditional forgiveness; a gift we don't deserve.'* 5 John 1:17 says that '... grace and truth came through Jesus Christ.' What do you think this means?

The whole of Jesus' life was characterised by the goodness of his perfection, mercy and grace, and these were best seen when he died on the cross as a substitute for sinners.

As you consider these characteristics, *take time now* to give thanks to the Lord for his goodness in going to the cross and giving up his life so that, by trusting in him, you are saved from the punishment and the power of sin.

The Holy Spirit and goodness

The word 'good' in the language of Scripture literally means 'to be like God', because He alone is the One who is perfectly good. It is one thing, however, to have high ethical standards but quite another for the Holy Spirit to produce the goodness that has its depths in the Godhead. The meaning here is more than just 'doing good'. Goodness goes far deeper. Goodness is love in action. It carries with it not only the idea of righteousness imputed, but righteousness demonstrated in everyday life living by the Holy Spirit. It is doing good out of a good heart, to please God, without expecting medals and rewards. Christ wants this kind of goodness to be the way of life for every Christian. Man can find no substitute for goodness, and no spiritual touch-up artist can imitate it.
Billy Graham 6

Although it's not possible for us to be perfect like Jesus as we live from day to day, it's amazing to realise that the Holy Spirit can produce the fruit of goodness in us if we allow him to be in charge of our lives. Ephesians 5:8–10 are lovely verses – I like what the New Living Translation says: *'For though your hearts were once full of darkness, now you are full of light from the Lord, and your behaviour should show it! For this light within you produces only what is good and right and true.'* These verses indicate that Christian believers have a responsibility to live out what they believe. One way they can do this is by reflecting the goodness of God to those around them. However, people who are not Christian believers often do good things. In what way(s) does their goodness differ from the goodness which is a fruit of the Spirit?

'The bright light of Christ makes your way plain. So no more stumbling around. Get on with it! The good, the right, the true – these are the actions appropriate for daylight hours. Figure out what will please Christ, and then do it.'
Ephesians 5:8,9 *The Message* 7

The Bible makes it clear that we can't become Christians by doing good things. In fact, unbelievers expecting to be allowed into heaven on the basis of the good things they've done is as inappropriate as dressing in filthy, torn clothes and expecting to be admitted to the Queen's garden party! (Isaiah 64:6).

Read Ephesians 2:8–10

Q Paul utterly refutes the notion that we can take pride in our works. He gives at least three reasons why there is no room for boasting. What are they?

Read James 2:14–26

Q God is concerned that those of us who are already Christians should turn our faith into action. 'What good is it, my brothers, if a man claims to have faith but has no deeds?' Why is it important that faith translates into action?

Read Matthew 7:15–20

Q Jesus teaches that a good tree is recognisable by its good fruit. Obedience cannot be feigned. Are there any areas of your life where you are 'going through the motions' of obedience?

Personal comment

As a child, I frequently got into trouble with my parents for doing something which displeased them. Often, I would respond by saying, 'I'll be good! I'll be good!' I thought all that was necessary was to act in an appropriate way and I would then be 'good'. I realise now that goodness or 'being good' isn't restricted to my outward behaviour. I know that my motives need to be right – if they're not, then any subsequent action I take will not be truly good. Jesus was good because his motives were right. What was his main motive as he lived and died? The answer can be found in John 6:38,39 – to do His Father's will, and not to satisfy his human desires. Do I have the same purpose? Do I want to do the will of God, even when I don't know what it is? Am I prepared to trust him unconditionally, believing that his will for me is good, because he is good? Or am I prepared to do his will only if it meets with my approval?

Goodness, as a fruit of the Spirit, doesn't stand alone. Look again at the verse at the start of this chapter which talks about the fruit of the light consisting of all goodness, righteousness and truth. In order for goodness to be produced in me, I need to be in a right relationship with God. This reminds me again that I need to remain close to Jesus. Truth is also an important companion here – I can't have a meaningful relationship with the Lord if I fail to acknowledge that he is the ultimate Truth (John 14:6). This means that I have to believe what he says in his Word – the Bible – and this should result in changes in my behaviour in order to bring my actions into line with his will for me.

Yesterday was the Sunday School prize-giving in church and it was lovely to hear the pre-school children singing: 'God is so good, God is so good, God is so good, He's so good to me.' Over the next few days, think about how good God is to you, and co-operate with the Holy Spirit so he can produce his fruit of goodness in you as you remain intimately in touch with Jesus Christ.

7| Faithfulness

'Great is His faithfulness; His mercies begin afresh each day.'
Lamentations 3:23 (NLT)

*To be faithful in every circumstance means that we have only one
loyalty, or object of our faith – the Lord Jesus Christ... The goal of
faithfulness is not that we will do work for God, but that He will be
free to do His work through us. God calls us to His service and places
tremendous responsibilities on us. He expects no complaining on our
part and offers no explanation on His part. God wants to use us as
He used His own Son.*
Oswald Chambers [1]

Do you have a borrowed book that you need to return? Did you promise
someone you would phone him and haven't yet done so? Have you been
unable to keep a secret recently? These are areas where we aren't always
as faithful as we should be, aren't they? Faithfulness isn't reserved only for
the big things like marriage partnerships – if we are going to be known as
loyal, dependable people who can be trusted with the small things in life
as well as the large, then we need to be faithful in *all* our relationships.
One definition states that *'faithfulness is being reliable in doing what you
should do.'* [2] Faithfulness is not something which is generally given high
priority in our society – success, prestige, and ambition often seem to be
much more valued. However, God has a lot to say about faithfulness. He is
a faithful God – always – and he wants his children to reflect the family
likeness. The Holy Spirit, therefore, wants to produce faithfulness as his
fruit in our lives.

The Father and faithfulness

We all fail the Lord; no one in His church is perfect. Yet every time we are unfaithful to Him, He remains faithful to us! So, take your eyes off your failures and weaknesses, and fix them on His faithfulness. He cannot deny Himself. He is utterly faithful to His word – and He is going to see you through all your battles! Hallelujah!
David Wilkerson [3]

How reassuring to know that God is faithful – that he never changes, that he is always true to his Word! How good to know also that he remains faithful, despite our faithlessness. Several verses in the Bible talk about God's faithfulness, and they make it clear to us that we are completely dependent on this aspect of his character. Look up the following references and match up the verses with the reasons why we need to depend on his faithfulness.

Verses	Reasons for dependence
Psalm 145:13	Forgiveness of our sins
Micah 7:18	Hope of eternal life
2 Corinthians 1:4,5	Help in temptation
Titus 1:2	Comfort in trouble
Hebrews 2:18	Fulfilment of his promises

All of these verses are a great encouragement to us as we think about the faithfulness of God. Why is it important that we depend on *his* faithfulness?

Read 2 Timothy 2:11–13

Q Pay particular attention to verse 13. For the encouragement of others in your study group, please share an example from your own experience where, despite your faithlessness, God has remained faithful to you.

The Lord Jesus Christ and faithfulness

Grant, O kind and beloved Jesus, that I may often think and meditate on these things; that I may believe on Thee, and cleave to Thee. May I never doubt Thy words and the truth eternal. In every temptation and sorrow, may I ever turn at once for comfort to Thy Passion, and seek for consolation in Thy sacred wounds and suffering. Yea, may I ever find peace and rest for my soul in Thee, Who, with the Father and the Holy Ghost, liveth and reigneth, ever one God, world without end. Amen.
Thomas à Kempis (1380–1471) 4

The faithfulness of Jesus can be seen in his single-minded determination to do the will of his Father.

Read John 4:34; John 17:4

Q Write down the main point of each verse.

Read John 6:37–40

Q This passage gives some information about what the Father's will is. How would you summarise the content?

Q What encouragement do these verses give you? Please share your answer with the rest of your study group.

Several verses in the Bible refer specifically to the faithfulness of the Lord Jesus Christ.

Read 2 Thessalonians 3:3; Hebrews 2:16,17; 1 John 1:9

Q Write down what each of the above passages say about the Lord being faithful.

Q Choose one of the above references which has particularly impressed you and give the reason(s) for your choice.

Take time to thank Jesus for being completely faithful to the will of his Father.

The Holy Spirit and faithfulness

I find that in the things I really like to do, I am as faithful as the day is long. I am unwavering. But, when it comes to the duties or obligations that are uncomfortable or boring, I usually find that my faithfulness can waver and I can come up with every excuse in the book as to why I just won't be able to do it ... If faithfulness is so important, I think we had better take it seriously.
Jan Silvious [5]

In the Bible, we read of the faithful example of Joseph in Egypt, of Daniel in Babylon, of Paul in prison. None of these people 'had it easy', yet all were faithful, not as a result of their own natural personalities, but because the Holy Spirit was at work producing the fruit of faithfulness in their lives. There are several ways in which, with the Spirit's help, we too can be faithful in our everyday lives. One of these ways is by being faithful to God's Word – we need to read it, believe it, and obey it.

Reading God's Word

Read Acts 17:11

Q Do you sometimes check what preachers say from the Bible?

Believing God's Word

Read John 20:31

Q How practically can we combine the message with faith (see Heb 4:2)?

Obeying God's Word

Read Psalm 119:8,34,67,129,168 (choose one or more of these verses or make your own choice from Psalm 119!)

Q In your own words, write out what each of these verses is saying.

Q Do you ever find it difficult to be faithful to God in any of the above three ways? Be specific, and outline practical steps you can take to overcome this.

The Bible has a lot to say about faithfulness in our relationships.

Read Proverbs 27:6; Ephesians 6:5–9; Colossians 3:18–21

Using one of the above verses, take time now to think about how you can apply it to your own situation.

> *We need to be faithful to our children. That's a part of our family. But being faithful to our friends I think is important too. Some people are faithful to their spouse, but not faithful to their job. Others are faithful to their job, but not faithful to their spouse. There are lots of ways for us to be faithful, but there is no greater way than being faithful to God. We need to live up to our promises to God and be pleasing to Him.*
> Woodrow Kroll [6]

Below is a list of statements connected with relationships. Put a tick beside those which demonstrate faithfulness.

◆ You feel that you would like to start your day with the Lord in prayer and Bible reading, so you decide to advance your alarm clock by twenty minutes. When the alarm goes off next morning, you ignore it and end up getting out of bed at your usual time.

◆ Before your next-door neighbour went on holiday, you promised him that you would remove any mail from behind his glass-fronted door. He has now been away almost two weeks and you haven't yet made it up his garden path.

◆ A friend tells you something which is confidential to her and asks that you don't pass it on to anyone else. You're tempted to mention some of the information to a mutual friend but decide against it.

◆ Your Bible study group has pledged to pray about a difficult situation in the church's youth club. Despite having numerous other prayer requests to respond to, your group decides to honour its commitment to pray for the young people.

◆ Your employer has praised you for your good time-keeping. You make sure that you are always at work on time on the days you know he is going to be in the office, but when he's away on business, you are not so careful about arriving promptly.

◆ You promised your children that you would take them to a theme park before the end of the summer holidays. They are now back at school and are still waiting for their day out.

◆ Your two friends have been married for several years and, despite having numerous opportunities, they have never broken their marriage vows.

Choose one of the above statements which you did *not* tick. From the verses below, select those which are relevant to the statement which you have chosen e.g. if you chose option 1, the relevant verses below are Psalm 63:1 and Mark 1:35.

Relationship with:

Your Lord

Read Psalm 63:1; Mark 1:35

Your neighbour

Read James 2:8; 1 John 3:18

Your employer

Read Colossians 3:22–24; Titus 2:9,10

Your children

Read Ecclesiastes 5:5; Ephesians 6:4

Q Suggest specific ways in which these verses could make a practical difference to the situation.

Personal comment

When James and I married, one of our wedding hymns was Great is Thy Faithfulness. *This hymn is based on Lamentations 3:23, and talks about the faithfulness of God and how his mercies are new every morning. Several years on, the words of the hymn are as true for us as they were when we sung them at our wedding. It is because God is faithful that he wants to see faithfulness in my relationship with him and with others. How faithful am I in reading God's Word (and I mean reading it willingly, eagerly, with a great desire to be shaped by what I read, and not reading it merely as a formal daily duty)? Am I faithful in believing that Word – always – or is there sometimes a feeling of unreality as I read and listen to the great truths of God? How faithful am I in obeying that Word – it's not too difficult to obey when what I read or hear fits in with my way of thinking, but what about the times when obedience means putting my own desires on hold – or even abandoning them altogether? And then, there's the matter of being faithful in my relationships with other people. Am I always loyal to my husband when I am speaking about him to a friend? Am I absolutely trustworthy in my professional life? Can my friends be certain that I will not gossip about them? Am I faithful in my church attendance and in giving my money, time and talents? Can I be relied upon to look after my neighbour's property when she is on holiday? Faithfulness touches every area of our lives, yet it is not a natural or a common quality – in Proverbs 20:6, we read that 'many will say they are loyal friends, but who can find one who is really faithful?' (NLT). The Holy Spirit desires to produce in me the fruit of faithfulness. As we go through this coming week, let's turn our attention towards the One who alone is truly faithful and, with the writer of Lamentations, let us say 'Great is his faithfulness; his mercies begin afresh each day.'*

8| Gentleness

'Let your gentleness be evident to all. The Lord is near.'

Philippians 4:5

In the book of Matthew, Jesus is described as 'gentle and mild.'
Although Jesus had the power to create the world, He controlled His
strength for the sake of others. Gentleness is holding back your
strength and your rights when it would be to another's benefit.
Jan Silvious [1]

Let me ask you a question – are you a gentle, meek person? I can almost
hear the protests: 'Meek? No way! Meekness is weakness. Who wants to be
a wimp?' Nothing, however, could be further from the truth. The general
idea of gentleness or meekness is not something negative, but 'power
under control'. I like the following statement (source unknown):
Gentleness is moderation in response to extremity, meekness in response to
condescension, humility in response to compliment, calmness in response to
anger. Gentleness is part of the character of God the Father; it is seen
perfectly in the life of Jesus; and it is produced by the Spirit in those who
remain in close relationship with the Lord.

The Father and gentleness

When we suffer any kind of relapse and breakdown, whether it be
physical, mental or spiritual, or whether it be a combination of all
three, the devil is very quick to come to us and say, 'You've had it!
…You can never be the same again after what has happened… Your
days of usefulness are over …!' But he is a liar! It is not true …fail-
ure is not final! Indeed, such is the grace and mysterious working of
God that He can take even our failures, our illnesses or our break-
downs, and He can use them in blessing to ourselves, and through us
to others, and thus use them for His glory.
Francis W Dixon [2]

If you were asked to describe God's character, how far up the list would you put the word 'gentle'? You know he is a God of love and peace; that he is majestic and holy; that he is all-powerful, all-knowing, and not restricted to any particular location – but did you know he is also *gentle*?

A good illustration of the gentleness of God is the way he dealt with the prophet Elijah. He had given Elijah great power – on Mount Carmel, in the strength of the Lord, Elijah defeated the prophets of Baal (1 Kings 18). Immediately following this, he prayed that God would send rain where there had been severe drought and his prayer was answered (18:45). Elijah then *ran* six miles from Mount Carmel to the city of Jezreel. It was at this point that wicked Queen Jezebel threatened to kill him (19:2). This was the last straw! Elijah fled for his life into the desert and in 1 Kings 19:4 he prayed that he would die. What does this sequence of events tell us about the relationship which sometimes exists between great spiritual experiences and severe breakdown?

Read 1 Kings 19:5–18

Q God gently led Elijah out of his depression. Outline the practical steps taken by God's angel in order to restore Elijah to a position of usefulness to God once again.

The Lord Jesus Christ and gentleness

Speaking of Isaiah 42:3, one author says:

> *Even at its best, a reed is weak, hollow, and fragile. A bruised reed depicts a spirit that is hanging on by a few threads. A smoldering wick depicts a spirit in which life and hope have all but vanished. Jesus, sent to reveal the nature of our Creator, was clothed in gentleness. This virtue allowed Him to enter into the lives of broken, hurting people.*
> Gary L Thomas [3]

In 2 Corinthians 10:1, the apostle Paul begins: *'By the meekness and gentle-*

ness of Christ ...' If we had no other Bible references to the gentleness of the Lord Jesus, this verse alone would tell us that he possessed meekness and gentleness. The use of the two words here might indicate a difference in their meaning. 'Meekness' conveys the idea of humility or submission. We have already seen in earlier chapters that Jesus' life was one of complete submission to his Father's will and all his actions could be understood in the light of that. 'Gentleness' carries with it the picture of showing a sensitive regard for other people. The following verses give examples of meekness and gentleness. Note that the Old Testament reference speaks prophetically about the Lord Jesus Christ.

Read Isaiah 42:3; Matthew 11:28–30; Matthew 21:5 (quoting from Zechariah 9:9)

Q Write down what each passage says about this aspect of the Lord's character.

Q Select one of the above passages which has made a particular impression on you and give the reason(s) for your choice.

Take time now to think carefully about your chosen verse and ask the Lord to help you to apply its truth to your circumstances.

The Holy Spirit and gentleness

Let's remind ourselves of some spiritual truths. Nobody, apart from God, is perfect. Your spouse will fail you. Your children will disappoint you. Your pastor won't meet your expectations. The time will come, therefore, when you will have a legitimate gripe. You will be right, and they will be wrong. This is the crossroads of gentleness. Which path will you take? Condemnation and censure or the application of unmerited favour? Before you make that decision, remind yourself of how God has treated you.
Gary L Thomas [4]

It's amazing to think that the Holy Spirit's desire is to produce in us the gentleness of Christ. We've already seen how 'meekness' and 'humility' can often be used interchangeably with 'gentleness'. Which word is used will sometimes depend on which translation of the Bible is being studied. The following references (from the NIV) speak to Christian believers about the importance of gentleness in their lives.

Read Philippians 4:5; Colossians 3:12; 1 Peter 3:15

Q In your own words, write down what each verse is saying.

Q If you had to select one of the above as your verse for the week, which one would you choose, and why?

Read 1 Timothy 6:11; 1 Peter 3:1–6

Q In 1 Timothy 6:11, *men* are encouraged to pursue gentleness. Christian *women* are specifically addressed in 1 Peter 3:1–6. Look at verses 3 and 4 of this chapter and write down what you understand by the phrase 'the unfading beauty of a gentle and quiet spirit'.

Q Why do you think this is an important quality for Christians to have?

The above two references make it clear that gentleness is not gendered – it is part of the Spirit's fruit which should be shown by men and women alike. Read the following imaginary stories and suggest how a Christian, relying on the power of the Spirit, might respond. Choose only one of your answers to share with the rest of your group.

◆ A woman comes home after a busy day at work to find that her husband has begun cooking the evening meal. She criticises him for messing up the kitchen and complains about his choice of vegetables. She finds fault with the music he's listening to as he prepares the food and then gets on to him for allowing the children to watch cartoons on television before doing their homework. Her husband knows she is being unreasonable, but he wants to respond in a Christ-like way. How might he show the fruit of gentleness to his wife in this situation?

◆ Isobel works beside a man who is difficult to get along with and he often taunts her about the fact that she is a Christian. He uses offensive language and seems to enjoy making her feel uncomfortable. Although she would prefer to work with a more agreeable person, Isobel realises that she might be the only Christian that her colleague will come into contact with and, so, she wants to respond appropriately. How might she show the fruit of gentleness to her colleague?

◆ Sheila is new to the area and lives alone. She first appeared at church three weeks ago and doesn't seem to know anyone yet. She strikes you as being very shy, as she hurries off home immediately after the services and doesn't stay for coffee. You want Sheila to feel welcome but don't want her to be overwhelmed with too much attention. You're convinced that a gentle approach is needed. How might you show the fruit of gentleness to Sheila?

Can you identify areas in your life where you know you don't exercise gentleness? Take time now to name these areas and ask the Lord to give you the willingness to co-operate with the Holy Spirit as he begins to grow this fruit in you. Thank him that he wants you to have a gentle and quiet spirit. As you stay close to him, and allow him to direct your life, this fruit of gentleness can be yours.

There are several things, however, which can disturb a gentle and quiet spirit. Look up the following verses and in the space provided make a note of the hindrance described.

Verses	Hindrances
Psalm 38:3	
Proverbs 29:22	
Matthew 6:25	
Mark 6:31	
Philippians 4:2,3	
Colossians 3:13	

Do you recognise any of these hindrances in your own life? If so, what suggestions for dealing with the problem can you share with the rest of your study group? Be as specific and as practical as you can.

Personal Comment

When I was a young child, my mother used to tell me a story about the sun and the wind. As she told the story, the images that came to my mind were very vivid and the sun and wind seemed to take on their own personalities! For those of you who don't know this story (and for those of you who do, but would be happy to hear it again), here it is.

The sun and the wind often argued about which of them was more powerful. The sun quietly insisted that he was, while the wind protested loudly that he had more power. One day the wind said to the sun, 'Do you see that man walking along the road? Whichever one of us can get him to take his coat off first will be the more powerful.' The sun was quite happy to go along with this.

The wind was the first to try to get the man to take his coat off. He blew short, strong bursts, thinking that his force would soon blow the man's coat off, but the man's response was to draw his coat tighter and tighter to himself. The wind moved up a gear or two and turned into a furious gale. 'This will get his coat off,' he said to the sun, 'and then we'll both know that I'm more powerful than you.' However, the man just wrapped his coat even more closely to himself. After all this effort, the wind eventually became exhausted and couldn't blow any more.

Then the sun came out and shone brightly on the man. He began to feel its warmth as he walked along the road. As he continued on his journey, the sun's rays beat down upon him to such an extent that, at last, he took his coat off in order to feel more comfortable.

Which one of the elements was shown to be the more powerful? In our dealings with other people, gentleness is like the sun, while aggression is like the wind. The former is indeed power under control.

In a similar vein, Billy Graham uses an illustration of sun melting an iceberg. He says, 'God's gentleness, or meekness, in us permits the rays of the sun of God's Holy Spirit to work on our icebound hearts, transforming them into instruments for good and for God. Spiritually, the gentle, Spirit-filled Christian is a prism through whom the rays of the sun's spectrum are gathered to minister to the icebergs of our carnality.' [5]

Our verse at the start of this chapter, from Philippians 4:5, states: 'Let your gentleness be evident to all. The Lord is near.' As you live through this week, will the warm sun of gentleness be your choice in all your relationships or will you choose the fierce wind of aggression? As you focus on our gentle God, trust the Holy Spirit to produce the fruit of gentleness in you.

9| Self-control

'A person without self-control is as defenceless as
a city with broken-down walls.'
Proverbs 25:28 (NLT)

*Self-control is the exercise of inner strength under the direction of
sound judgement that enables us to do, think, and say the things that
are pleasing to God.*
Jerry Bridges [1]

Are you a 'control freak'? Do you like to exercise a large amount of control
over other people or situations? Control freaks can be manipulative and
are not content unless everything is done their way. Such people,
however, may know little of self-control – *'the ability to resist immediate
gratification for the sake of a higher goal.'* [2] An important aspect of self-
control is the ability to exercise restraint in your behaviour. It is from this
perspective that we'll consider God's self-control, before looking at examples of self-control in the life of the Lord Jesus Christ, and practical ways in
which the Holy Spirit helps Christians to demonstrate this fruit in their
everyday lives.

The Father and self-control

*As we live like Jesus before others we will overflow with seeds of
truth, faith, love, and hope... It only takes a seed. God turns seeds
into fruitbearing trees every season.*
Mark R Littleton [4]

There are several examples in the Bible where we read of God the Father
exercising self-control or restraint. For example, he restrained his anger
and judgement in dealing with Cain after he murdered his brother, Abel

(Genesis 4:11–15). God also exercised self-control regarding the timing of Jesus' birth (Galatians 4:4,5). One of the greatest examples of his self-control was when Jesus was suffering humiliation, abuse and torture in the events leading up to, and including, the crucifixion.

Read Isaiah 53:4–6; John 3:16

Q Why do you think God restrained himself from delivering Jesus from the cross?

Take time now to consider what it must have cost God to exercise such self-control and thank him that his love and self-restraint are so closely linked.

God continues to show self-control and restraint in today's world. He doesn't react impulsively to the sinfulness of human behaviour. If you or I were in the position of God, we would probably have wiped out the human race long ago! Although the Bible teaches that God will judge the world and not everyone will be saved, why do you think he restrains himself from pouring out his judgement at the present time? You might find 1 Peter 3:9 helpful as you answer.

Do you care if people perish? Do you want them to come to repentance? Take time now to ask the Lord to give you a genuine concern for those who don't yet know him and take whatever steps are necessary to help bring them into his kingdom. For example:

◆ Pray persistently that particular individuals will become real Christians

◆ Be willing to talk about Jesus to others

◆ Get involved in your church's outreach programme

◆ Be ready to answer people's questions about your own beliefs

◆ Take care how you live.

The Lord Jesus Christ and self-control

Jesus loved this family and often stayed with them. He knew their pain but did not respond immediately. His delay had a specific purpose. God's timing, especially His delays, may make us think He is not answering or is not answering the way we want. But He will meet all our needs according to His perfect schedule and purpose (Philippians 4:19). Patiently await His timing.
Life Application Study Bible [4]

The Lord Jesus Christ was no stranger to self-control. He needed it to get up early in the morning after an exhausting time of ministry the night before (Mark 1:32–35). He showed it when he was tempted by the devil, and never sinned. His self-control was probably at its highest on the cross of Calvary, as he gave himself freely to unimaginable suffering. There are many other examples in the life of Jesus, but one episode which can teach us a lot is in chapter 11 of the Gospel of John – the account of the illness, death and resurrection of Jesus' friend, Lazarus.

Read John 11:1–45

Q In verses 5 and 6, we read that Jesus loved this family from Bethany, yet when he heard that Lazarus was ill, he stayed away for a further two days. Why do you think the Lord exercised such self-control in this instance?

Q Who benefited from this example of the Lord's self-control?

Q In what way(s) did they benefit?

The Holy Spirit and self-control

Ephesians 4:29 may be a small nugget of a verse, but it contains a huge amount of gold ... It would be an impossible command – for me at least – except for one thing: God never gives a command that He doesn't give the ability, in the power of the Holy Spirit, to do. Therefore, the ability to speak in a way that will benefit those we are talking to is possible. For some of us, it takes much more prayer, thought, and study than for others who seem to be born with discretion. However, God gives this command to every one of us in the Body of Christ – thereby assuring that the ability to speak wisely will be given even to me.
Carole Mayhall 5

Are you a self-controlled person? Your answer will depend on whether or not you are a Spirit-controlled person.

Ask yourself if there are areas in your life where you find it difficult to exercise self-control. List these areas and pray specifically that each item on your list will be brought under the control of the Holy Spirit. In many cases, this will take some time, so keep praying, day after day! The more of your life you allow the Spirit to influence, the more he will produce in you the fruit of self-control. Several verses in the Bible talk about self-control.

Read Proverbs 13:3; 1 Peter 5:8; 2 Peter 1:5–8

Q Write down in your own words what each passage says about the importance of the fruit of self-control.

There are several areas in which we need to exercise self-control. For example, we need to be self-controlled:

◆ In our attitude towards money and in how we spend it, knowing that we are accountable to God for how we use the resources he has given to us

◆ In all areas of sexual temptation

◆ In the time we give to reading the Bible and to praying

◆ In dealing with anger to prevent it from becoming sinful

◆ In our speech, and this is the area of self-control which we are going to look at for the remainder of this chapter.

Read Ephesians 4:29

Q This verse sums up the way we should use speech. Write down both the negative and the positive commands which are given.

Lack of self-control in our speech can be seen in many ways, eg gossiping; grumbling and complaining; and talking when we should be silent. All of these can have far-reaching consequences for other people.

Read Proverbs 18:8

Q How would you define 'gossip' and in what way is it like 'choice morsels'?

Read Proverbs 26:20

Q See if you can put the practical wisdom of this proverb into your own words.

It is as hard to refuse to listen to gossip as it is to turn down a delicious dessert. Taking just one morsel of either one creates a taste for more. You can resist rumours the same way a determined dieter resists (chocolate) – never even open the box. If you don't nibble on the first bite of gossip, you can't take the second and the third.
Life Application Study Bible 6

Another way in which our speech can be negative is by grumbling or complaining. Exodus 14:11,12 records the first instance of grumbling and complaining by the Israelites.

Read Exodus 14:11,12

Q What can you learn from this example of the Israelites' lack of faith in God?

Q How might you use this knowledge in dealing with a grumbling or complaining spirit in your own life?

Read Philippians 2:14-16

Q The apostle Paul is writing to church members and urges them to avoid complaints and arguments. Write down the reasons given for this instruction.

Q Why are complaining and arguing so harmful in church relationships? What can you do to avoid this?

Whenever we have a recurring 'speech problem', we need to look for its source. If we're perpetually complaining, it's likely we've never learned to be thankful, or to obey God's command to focus on the good and beautiful things around us (Philippians 4:8). On an even deeper level, we may be trying to wrest control of our lives from God, demanding that things go our way and resisting the circumstances He brings into our lives for our good.
Susan Maycinik 7

Sometimes the most appropriate form of speech control is to say nothing at all. Often, we can be uncomfortable with silence and feel we need to say something – anything – in order to feel at ease. The Bible guides us in the important issue of keeping quiet, as well as giving us advice about waiting and thinking before speaking. Read the verses below and match them up with the appropriate descriptions.

Verses	Descriptions
Proverbs 10:19	Discern the need for speech or silence
Proverbs 15:28a	Silence before chief priests and elders
Ecclesiastes 3:7	Consider speech before opening mouth
Matthew 27:12–14	Say nothing

Do you find it difficult to get a balance between speech and silence? Do you want your words to build others up and not bring them down?

Read Isaiah 50:4

As you read the opening words of Isaiah 50, ask the Lord to make them true of you.

Personal comment

I find it quite a challenge to know when to be silent! When I was in my very first year of school, I was told to stand outside the classroom door as a punishment for talking when I should have been quiet. I was puzzled by this and said to the teacher, 'But I talk all the time at home!' I had yet to learn the truth of Ecclesiastes 3:1,7: 'There is a time for everything … a time to be silent and a time to speak.' Do you exercise self-control by remaining silent when a thoughtless response from you would deeply hurt someone? Are you self-controlled when someone criticises you? How self-controlled are you when you are on the point of becoming involved in a senseless argument? What about the areas of self-control that we didn't consider in this chapter – anger, money, sex, prioritising time for Bible study and prayer? Without self-control, I'm open to all sorts of sinful traps – I'm 'as defenseless as a city with broken-down walls' (Proverbs 25:28).

A self-controlled person is a Spirit-controlled person and a Spirit-controlled person is a self-controlled person. The Holy Spirit will not force himself on us – we can choose whether or not we will give him access to all areas of our lives. If there is an area in your life which is not under the Spirit's control, you won't be self-controlled in that area. As I continue to submit to the Spirit's authority in my life, by obeying the commands of the Lord and by remaining in close relationship with him, he will be pleased to produce his fruit in me – and the fruit of the Spirit is ... self-control.

10| **Keep growing!**

'Yes, I am the vine; you are the branches. Those who remain in me, and I in them, will produce much fruit. For apart from me you can do nothing.'

John 15:5 (NLT)

When we are consistently walking with the Lord and allowing the Holy Spirit to control us, precious fruit will be produced. This happens as we understand that Jesus is the Vine, and we are the branches. A branch must stay connected to the Vine if it is to bear fruit. And that is all the branch has to do! As we stay joined to our Lord, His life will begin to flow through us ... Your bearing fruit brings glory to God, builds the body of Christ, and brings others to the Saviour. Your fruit is evidence of your journey to the heart of God, and it will bring you much joy in the Lord.

Cynthia Heald [1]

I think it's exciting to realise that when we show evidence of the fruit of the Spirit in our lives, we're showing nothing less than the character of God! We've seen in this study that the Holy Spirit produces his fruit in us if we stay in touch with Jesus Christ by loving and obeying him. In John 15:1–8, Jesus illustrates this by painting a word picture for us. Here it is in the New Living Translation.

'I am the true vine, and my Father is the gardener. He cuts off every branch that doesn't bear fruit, and he prunes the branches that do bear fruit so they will produce even more. You have already been pruned for greater fruitfulness by the message I have given you. Remain in me, and I will remain in you. For a branch cannot produce fruit if it is severed from the vine, and you cannot be fruitful apart from me. Yes, I am the vine; you are the branches. Those who remain in me, and I in them, will produce much fruit. For apart from me you can do nothing. Anyone who parts from me is thrown away like a useless branch and withers. Such branches are gathered into a pile to be burned. But if you stay joined to me and my words remain in you, you may ask any request you like, and it will be granted! My true disciples produce much fruit. This brings great glory to my Father.' 2

Get connected!

Christ is the vine, and God is the gardener who cares for the branches to make them fruitful. The branches are all those who claim to be followers of Christ. The fruitful branches are true believers who by their living union with Christ produce much fruit. But those who become unproductive – those who turn back from following Christ after making a superficial commitment – will be separated from the vine. Unproductive followers are as good as dead and will be cut off and tossed aside.
Life Application Study Bible 3

Jesus often made use of imagery to get important truths across to his hearers. In John 15, he used the illustration of a grapevine – a picture that would be quite familiar to those listening to him in first century Jerusalem.

Read John 15:1,2 (NIV)

Q Identify who/what are represented by the following words: vine, gardener, unfruitful branches, fruitful branches.

Q Like the unfruitful branches, it's possible to have a 'connection' with the Lord Jesus Christ which does not lead to salvation. What examples of this can you give?

Is your connection to Jesus real and living or is it just a pretence? Have you ever cried out to him for forgiveness from your sins and to bring you into a right relationship with him? If not, ask him now to make the connection real – He won't turn you away (John 6:37). He'll give you his Holy Spirit to help you live in a way that pleases him. For more information about this important matter, you might find it helpful to speak to your group leader.

Even though withered branches may have some appearances of the living branches, they are discarded for they are lifeless. Artificial flowers and fruit may look much like the real ones, but an artificial apple is not pleasing to the palate or satisfying. Luscious fruit is possible only through a vital relationship to the vine and through the continuing attention of the gardener who daily inspects the vineyard.
David L Larsen [4]

Stay in touch!

A branch is good for only one thing – bearing fruit. It may be weak in itself, but it has a living relationship with the vine and can be productive. To abide in Christ means to be in communion with Him so that our lives please Him. We know that we are abiding when the Father prunes us, cutting away the good so that we can produce the best. We glorify God with fruit, more fruit, much fruit.
Warren W Wiersbe [5]

To be healthy, a branch must be connected to the main part of the tree so that the nourishment from the sap will flow from it to the branch. The same is true of Christian believers and their Lord. We must stay in touch with him to enjoy spiritual nourishment. In order to appreciate what it means to stay vitally connected to Jesus, look up the following selection of references and match the verse with the appropriate principle of staying in touch.

Verses	Principle of staying in touch
Psalm 119:97	Don't give up meeting with other Christians
John 1:12	Believing that Jesus is the Son of God
John 13:34,35	Becoming a child of God
1 Corinthians 11:23–26	Loving other believers
Philippians 4:6	Being obedient to God's commands
Hebrews 10:25	Studying God's Word
1 John 2:24	Praying with thanksgiving
1 John 3:24	Continuing to believe the gospel
1 John 4:15	Remembering Jesus' sacrifice

Which of these principles do you find particularly difficult? Group members might be able to offer some practical suggestions to help you with this.

We need more quiet fellowship with God. I tell you in the name of the heavenly Vine that you cannot be a healthy branch, a branch into which the heavenly sap can flow, unless you take plenty of time for communion with God. If you are not willing to sacrifice time to get alone with Him, to give Him time every day to work in you, to keep up the link of connection between you and Himself, He cannot give you that blessing of His unbroken fellowship. Jesus Christ asks you to live in close communion with Him. Let every heart say: 'O Christ, it is this I long for, it is this I choose.' And He will gladly give it to you.
Andrew Murray 6

In the same way as a gardener prunes or cuts back branches from a favourite shrub or tree in order to encourage new growth, our loving heavenly Father takes care to prune us too. This can be a painful, but necessary, process if our lives are to be fruitful.

Read Hebrews 12:11; James 1:2,3; 1 Peter 1:6,7

Q Write down what each verse says about pruning, or disciplining, by God.

Q From your own experience, can you share a particular time of pruning which, although difficult to bear at the time, resulted in you becoming more fruitful?

The branches that are fruitful must be trimmed drastically and deliberately. The pruning instrument is the Word of God (John 15:3), 'sharper than any double-edged sword' (Hebrews 4:12). Maximum yield requires severe pruning. The process may be acutely painful, but it is through chastening that we realise 'a harvest of righteousness and peace' (Hebrews 12:11). The process is purposeful, and we must never forget that the pruning knife is in the Father's hand.
David I Larsen 7

Be fruitful!

Any other trait commended in Scripture as befitting a believer is also a fruit of the Spirit, since its evidence is a result only of the Spirit's ministry in our hearts. So, to the qualities listed in Galatians 5 – love, joy, peace, patience, kindness, goodness, faithfulness, gentleness, and self-control – we can also add such traits as holiness, humility, compassion, forbearance, contentment, thankfulness, considerateness, sincerity, and perseverance.
Jerry Bridges 8

Christian believers are people who have the Holy Spirit living in them. They remain vitally connected to their Lord as they stay in touch with him from day to day. It's through this connection that they gain spiritual nourishment as the Holy Spirit produces his fruit in their lives. Although they may have a long way to go before his fruit is seen in every area of their lives, there will still be evidence that they belong to the Lord as they display, in some measure, the fruit of the Spirit.

Throughout this study, we've looked in some detail at the spiritual fruit listed in Galatians 5:22,23. However, this isn't the only fruit referred to in the Bible.

Read Psalm 92:12–15 (particularly verse 14); Philippians 1:9–11 (particularly verse 11); Hebrews 13:15

Q For your encouragement write down what each verse says about bearing fruit.

Q Choose one of the above passages and say how you can put its teaching into practice.

Q In what other way(s) can you bear fruit?

Read John 15:8

In what way(s) can bearing much fruit:

Glorify our Father in heaven?

Show that we are Christ's disciples?

Take time now to ask the Lord for his help as you continue to commit yourself to an ongoing, close relationship with him. Praise him that 'He who began a good work in you will carry it on to completion ...' (Philippians 1:6). Thank him for giving you his Spirit who wants to produce his fruit in your life.

Someone recently handed me this about the fruit of the Spirit: 'Joy is love singing. Peace is love resting. Long-suffering is love enduring. Kindness is love remaining with patience. Goodness is love's character. Faithfulness is love's habit. Meekness is love's true touch. Self-control is love holding the reins. But the greatest of these is love.'
William Still 9

Personal comment

I'm so glad that the fruit of the Spirit is just that – it belongs to the Spirit and trying to produce spiritual fruit on my own is just not going to work. What then is my responsibility? If it's all down to what the Holy Spirit does in my life, do I need to do anything at all? I think that John 15:5 helps us to answer these questions.

'Yes, I am the vine; you are the branches.' Jesus reminds us that He is the source of spiritual power and nourishment, and we are the branches. Do you ever find yourself thinking that you are the vine and are therefore able to produce fruit without any help from the Holy Spirit or anyone else? Maybe that's why we fail so often and the fruit we produce shrivels up in the heat of everyday life.

'Those who remain in me, and I in them, will produce much fruit.' Our relationship with the Lord is two-way – we have to remain in him by loving him and obeying him, and he has promised that he will remain in us by his Spirit. With this partnership in place, we can co-operate with the Holy Spirit as he produces his fruit in our lives. As we stay in touch with Jesus, willing to obey him and be changed by his Spirit within us, the spiritual fruit of Galatians 5:22,23 can begin to be produced. Our responsibility is to remain vitally connected to Jesus and allow his power to work in us – in his way, not ours. Colossians 1:29 gives us a picture of this sort of co-operation. The apostle Paul talks about warning and teaching others about the importance of having a living relationship with the Lord. He says 'I work very hard at this (human side), as I depend on Christ's mighty power that works within me' (divine side) – New Living Translation.

'For apart from me you can do nothing'. This suggests that we can't bear lasting spiritual fruit by our own efforts. Are you willing to give up your independence and doing things your own way in your own strength? Are you

prepared to give the Lord permission to produce his fruit in you, transforming you so that you become more like Jesus?

If we want to be fruitful, we can't do it on our own – neither will the Holy Spirit do it for us on his own. Will you co-operate with him in the fruit-production process by giving up your own agenda, and allow him to work in and through you in the way he wants? Even a hesitant 'Yes' can be the beginning of great things in the power of the Spirit – be fruitful!

Endnotes

Chapter 1

1 Jan Silvious, *The 5-Minute Devotional*, Zondervan, 1991, p44.

2 James Aderman, *Fruit of the Spirit – Love.*
   www.wels.net/sab/listen/bs-fruit1.html

3 James I Packer, *Knowing God*, Hodder & Stoughton, 1973, p41.
   Reproduced with the permission of Hodder & Stoughton Limited.

4 John R W Stott, *The Cross of Christ*, IVP, 1986, p212.

5 Samuel Trevor Francis, 'O the deep, deep love of Jesus', first verse, in
   Christian Hymns, Evangelical Movement of Wales, 1997, no. 143.

6 Cynthia Heald, *Abiding in Christ: A Month of Devotionals*, NavPress, 1995,
   p12.

7 Anne Meskey Elhajoui, 'What's The Big Deal About Love?' *Discipleship
   Journal*, no. 79 (Jan/Feb 1994). (Text taken from CD Rom, published by
   NavPress. Visit www.discipleshipjournal.org for details.)

8 Oswald Chambers, *My Utmost For His Highest*, Oswald Chambers
   Publications Association Ltd, 1927, 11 May.

Chapter 2

1 De Vern F Fromke, *The Ultimate Intention*, CLC, 1963, 1980, p115.

2 Max Anders, *What You Need To Know About The Holy Spirit In 12 Lessons*,
   Thomas Nelson, 1995, p151.

3 Matthew Henry, *Concise Commentary on the Whole Bible*, Moody Press,
   1983.

4 Oswald Chambers, *My Utmost For His Highest*, Oswald Chambers
   Publications Association Ltd, 1927.

5 Warren and Ruth Myers, *Praise: A Door to God's Presence*, NavPress, 1987,
   p155.

6 Warren W Wiersbe, *The Bumps Are What You Climb On*, Crossway Books, 1980, p116.

7 Cynthia Heald, *Abiding in Christ: A Month of Devotionals*, NavPress, 1995, pp53,54.

Chapter 3

1 Max Anders, *What You Need To Know About The Holy Spirit In 12 Lessons*, Thomas Nelson, 1995, p154.

2 Max Anders *What You Need To Know About The Holy Spirit In 12 Lessons*, Thomas Nelson, 1995, p153.

3 Charles Spurgeon, *Cheque Book Of The Bank Of Faith*, Christian Focus, 1996, 16 March.

4 Oswald Chambers, *My Utmost For His Highest*, Oswald Chambers Publications Association Ltd, 1927.

5 Billy Graham, *The Holy Spirit*, Marshall Pickering, 1995, p205.

6 Elisabeth Elliot, *A Heart for God, Gateway to Joy*, 1995, 23 July.

7 Lorraine Pintus, 'At Peace in the Whirlwind', *Discipleship Journal*, no. 97 (Jan/Feb 1997). (Text taken from CD Rom, published by NavPress. Visit www.discipleshipjournal.org for details.)

8 Neil Anderson, *Walking in the Light*, Monarch, 1993, p123.

Chapter 4

1 Billy Graham, *The Holy Spirit*, Marshall Pickering, 1995, p206,207.

2 Mary Whelchel in 'Learning to Wait', (audio cassette) *The Christian Working Woman*, May 1999. (This organisation broadcasts in the USA and elsewhere. See www.christianworkingwoman.org for transcripts.)

3 Cynthia Heald, *Abiding in Christ: A Month of Devotionals*, NavPress, 1995, p42.

4 Thomas à Kempis, *Meditations on the Life of Christ*, Baker Book House, 1978, p154.

5 Matthew Henry, *Concise Commentary on the Whole Bible*, Moody Press, 1983, p329.

6 Robert Jamieson, A R Fausset, and David Brown, *Commentary on the Whole Bible*, Zondervan, p1149.

Chapter 5

1 Cole Huffman, 'Trash or Treasure?' *Discipleship Journal*, no. 118 (July/Aug 2000), p28.

2 Max Anders, *What You Need To Know About The Holy Spirit In 12 Lessons*, Thomas Nelson, 1995, p162.

3 Eugene H Peterson, *The Message*, NavPress, 1993, p306.

4 Helene Ashker, *Jesus Changes Women*, NavPress, 1997, p31.

5 Jan Silvious, *The Five Minute Devotional – Meditations for the Busy Woman*, Zondervan Publishing House, 1991, pp74,75.

6 Ruth Bell Graham, 'The One I Missed', *Decision Magazine*, May 1999. www.decisionmag.org

7 Ruth Bell Graham, 'The One I Missed', *Decision Magazine*, May 1999. www.decisionmag.org

Chapter 6

1 James Aderman, Fruit of the Spirit – Goodness. www.wels.net/sab/listen/bs-fruit6.html

2 *Life Application Study Bible: New Living Translation*, Tyndale House Publishers Inc, 1996, p2196.

3 Joseph Hart, 'How good is the God we adore', first verse, in *Christian Hymns*, Evangelical Movement of Wales, 1997, no. 575.

4 A W Tozer, *The Attributes of God*, Christian Publications, 1997, p101.

5 Jim and Karen Covell, Victorya Michaels Rogers, *How To Talk About Jesus Without Freaking Out*, Multnomah Publishers, Inc., 2000, p118.

6 Billy Graham, *The Holy Spirit*, Marshall Pickering, 1995, p212.

7 Eugene H Peterson, *The Message*, NavPress, 1997, p408.

Chapter 7

1 Oswald Chambers, *My Utmost For His Highest*, Oswald Chambers Publications Association Ltd, 1927, 18 December.

2 Max Anders, *What You Need To Know About The Holy Spirit In 12 Lessons*, Thomas Nelson, 1995, p166.

3 David Wilkerson, *God Is Faithful – Even When We Are Not!*, Times Square Church Pulpit Series, 22 January 1996. tscpulpitseries.org

4 Thomas à Kempis, *Meditations on the Life of Christ*, Baker Book House, 1978.

5 Jan Silvious, *The Five-Minute Devotional – Meditations for the Busy Woman*, Zondervan, 1991, p65.

6 Woodrow Kroll, 'Back to the Bible', internet broadcast 22 March 1999. www.backtothebible.org

Chapter 8

1 Jan Silvious, *The Five-Minute Devotional – Meditations for the Busy Woman*, Zondervan, 1991, p34.

2 Francis W Dixon, *Elijah's God and Mine*, Lakeland, 1978, pp72–3.

3 Gary L Thomas, *The Glorious Pursuit*, NavPress, 1998. Used with permission. All rights reserved.

4 Gary L Thomas, *The Glorious Pursuit*, NavPress, 1998. Used with permission. All rights reserved.

5 Billy Graham, *The Holy Spirit*, Marshall Pickering, 1995, p220.

Chapter 9

1 Jerry Bridges, *The Practice of Godliness*, NavPress, 1996, p134.

2 Max Anders, *What You Need To Know About The Holy Spirit In 12 Lessons*, Thomas Nelson, 1995, p169.

3 Mark R Littleton, 'Plant Seeds, Not Burning Bushes', *Discipleship Journal*, no. 25 (Jan/Feb 1985). (Text taken from CD Rom, published by NavPress. Visit www.discipleshipjournal.org for details.)

4 *Life Application Study Bible: New Living Translation*, Tyndale House, 1996, p1646.

5 Carole Mayhall, 'Words of the Wise', *Discipleship Journal*, no. 94 (Jul/Aug 1996), p46.

6 *Life Application Study Bible: New Living Translation*, Tyndale House, 1996, p1004.

7 Susan Maycinik, 'Why Did I Say That?', *Discipleship Journal*, no. 94 (Jul/Aug 1996), p42.

Chapter 10

1 Cynthia Heald, *A Woman's Journey To The Heart Of God*, Thomas Nelson, 1997, pp194, 201.

2 *New Living Translation*, Tyndale House, 1996, p1657–8.

3 *Life Application Study Bible: New Living Translation*, Tyndale House, 1996, p1657.

4 David L Larsen, 'Jesus: The True Vine – Living in Christ', *Decision Magazine*, June 1999. www.decisionmag.org

5 Warren W Wiersbe, *With The Word – The Chapter-by-Chapter Bible Handbook*, Thomas Nelson, 1991, p700.

6 Andrew Murray, *The Believer's Absolute Surrender*, Bethany House Publishers, 1985, p151.

7 David L Larsen, 'Jesus: The True Vine – Living in Christ', *Decision Magazine*, June 1999. www.decisionmag.org

8 Jerry Bridges, *The Practice of Godliness*, NavPress, 1983, 1996, p57.

9 William Still, *Collected Writings of William Still – Volume 1: Theological Studies*, Rutherford House, 1990, p154.

Other Resources from Scripture Union

Bodybuilders

Small group resource

A highly relational small group resource that's flexible and fun to use. Six outlines in each book contain notes for leaders, prayer and worship ideas, photocopiable sheets of interactive and in-depth Bible study material and ideas for personal study during the week.

A Fresh Encounter (David Bolster) 1 85999 586 1

Designed for Great Things (Anton Bauhmohl) 1 85999 585 3

Living for the King (Tricia Williams) 1 85999 584 5

Relationship Building (Lance Pierson) 1 85999 582 9

Surviving Under Pressure (Christopher Griffiths & Stephen Hathway) 1 85999 587 X

Growing Through Change (Lance Pierson) 1 85999 583 7

210x140mm pb 32pp   £3.50

Understanding the Bible

John Stott

A format pb 192pp £2.99

ISBN 1 85999 225 0

A special budget edition of a widely-acclaimed classic bestseller. Outstanding Christian teacher and author John Stott examines the cultural, social, geographical and historical background of the Bible, outlining the story and explaining the message.

Understanding the Bible

John Stott

245x160mm hb 170pp £9.99

1 85999 569 1

A brand new edition in full colour. Revised and updated text is illustrated with charts, diagrams and wonderful colour photos. An ideal gift!

Christian Life and Today's World package

(Video editor: Rob Purbrick)

ISBN 1 85999 576 4

How can we take up the challenge of living as Christians in a postmodern society? From SU and LBC comes another stimulating small group resource containing video, accompanying workbook for group leaders and book of articles written by members of the LBC faculty.

A format pb 192pp + workbook 60pp + video £25.00

Light from a Dark Star

Where's God when my world falls apart?

Wayne Kirkland

ISBN: 1 85999 515 2, £4.99

It's the big question that won't go away. Why does God allow suffering? There are no simple answers in this book. No attempts to shrug off the serious challenges to faith which the question raises. Rather it engages compassionately with the sufferings of real people, grappling with slippery issues, in a discovery of some intriguing perspectives.

Knowing God's Ways

A user's guide to the Old Testament

Patton Taylor

ISBN: 1 85999 349 4, £6.99

Do you find the Old Testament difficult to get into? If you've been looking for some help in making sense of it all, then this book by a professor at Union Theological College in Belfast is what you've been looking for! His accessible. user-friendly approach will help you gain a clear overview of the Old Testament, understand different genres, and apply biblical teaching to today's world.

Journey into the Bible

John Drane

ISBN: 1 85999 409 1, £4.99

In his usual thought-provoking and accessible style John Drane gives a stimulating introduction to many of the issues raised by reading the Bible today. Designed especially for those who are struggling to come to terms with the Bible.

Dangerous Praying

Inspirational Ideas for individuals and groups

David Spriggs

ISBN: 1 85999335 4, £6.99

Drawing on Paul's letter to the Ephesians, this creative book challenges us to be bold when we pray, both in what we pray for and how we pray. David Spriggs presents us with 101 practical ideas and strategies to help us develop a courageous prayer life, whether in a group or individually.

Ready to Grow

Practical steps to knowing God better

Alan Harkness

ISBN 0 949720 71 2, £5.99

An attractive and practical book to encourage believers to make time with God a regular part of their lives. Includes chapters on preparation, getting started, the practicalities, sharing what you have learned, and different methods of combining Bible reading and prayer.

Faith and Common Sense

Living boldly, choosing wisely

David Dewey

ISBN: 1 85999 302 8, £4.99

This unusual book explores how we can live riskily yet sensibly. Drawing on the lives of key Bible characters like Peter, the author first lays a solid biblical and theological foundation for achieving a balance. Then follows a practical look at areas in our lives where a need for that balance is vital - healing, the gifts of the Spirit, work, money, failure and guidance.

The Bible Unwrapped

Developing your Bible skills

David Dewey

ISBN: 1 85999 533 0, £5.99

Is the Bible something of a closed book to you? Here you'll find help in finding your way around the Bible, and in grasping the big picture of the Bible's message. You'll also learn to appreciate the different types of literature in the Bible and be introduced to eight different approaches to Bible study. Clear and accurate charts and diagrams and a helpful glossary add value.